An Essential H
Managers and Em

POTENTIAL

Find it. Own it. Work it.

DAVID GUILE

Praise

'It is said that you cannot buy experience, but this book disproves that theory and challenges many others. You will not buy a more intuitive or more genuinely helpful leadership book.'
Stephanie Hocking, CEO, Andrew Brownsword Hotels

'A powerful read for all managers and emerging leaders within the hospitality sector. This book will help you embrace and fulfil your own potential – and just as importantly, the potential of others within the industry.'
Ufi Ibrahim, CEO, British Hospitality Association

'You won't find a more potent book than *Potential*. Whether you're just starting out or already in a leadership role, it's packed full of useful exercises, coaching tools and business insights that will positively impact your own behaviour and influence others.'
Danny Pecorelli, Managing Director, Exclusive Hotels and Venues

'This book is like having a very practical business coach with you at all times, helping you question what you're doing and supporting you to achieve your best. David Guile draws on recognised coaching and business practices, packaging it all up into a book that is easy to read and easy to put into practice.'
Anne Scoular, Co-founder and faculty member of Meyler Campbell, author of *The Financial Times Guide to Business Coaching*

'Potential is a great read. It's well structured with just the right balance between theory and David's experiences, based on his successful career of over 25 years leading to CEO. This book is written in a practical, helpful and humble way. Importantly, it's grounded in the real world of work. You can't help but reflect and question, "Am I doing all I can to perform at my absolute best?" For many of us I would suggest the answer is No. If so, this book is for you.'

Tracy Robbins, Executive Leadership Coach and former EVP Global HR & Group Board Member, Intercontinental Hotel Group

'The ideal book to support and enhance the professional development of my management team.'

Richard Mayne, General Manager, Radisson Blu Edinburgh

REƎHINK PRESS

First published in Great Britain 2017
by Rethink Press (www.rethinkpress.com)
© Copyright David Guile

Table of Contents

*To Jemma and Hannah
and your potential*

Introduction

This book is written to help you find, own and fulfil your potential, and in turn help your team, your business or your department to find, own and fulfil their potential. Drawing on my personal experiences and learnings, and combining the principles and tools from a business and coaching perspective, I explore the key areas that can support personal and team growth and development.

I have enjoyed over twenty-five years'service within the hotel and hospitality sector having started my career as a hotel trainee within Forte Hotels and then steadily worked my way up through various managerial roles to eventually CEO and Board level within Macdonald Hotels and Resorts.

I have worked alongside and led many teams during my career, and have been fortunate to be able to influence the performance of individuals and encourage and support many to greater success within their careers – as others have done for me. However, not everyone achieves their true potential despite their best efforts and the efforts of others, and many of us are capable of much more than we realise.

By following my passion of seeing people grow and develop within their careers I am now working as an Executive Leadership Coach, supporting individuals and businesses to realise and fulfill their potential and to achieve their goals and ambitions.

You may have questions about how you and your team can achieve your potential. Perhaps you see others getting on and being promoted while you are stuck at a particular level within your career.

Are you brimming with confidence and want to channel your energies into maximising your potential and creating opportunities for yourself? Are you leading a team of people and want to get the best out of them? Are you aware of your strengths yet unsure how to use them to create a competitive advantage for you and your team?

Read on to discover how to:

- Become more successful in your career
- Become a more effective and dynamic leader whom others want to work for
- Gain clarity in terms of what you want and how to achieve it
- Enhance your positivity, self-belief and confidence
- Take control of yourself and positively influence the future.

Here's the framework to help you Find, Own and Work your Potential.

The Dynamics of Potential

The Dynamics of Potential is a business model aimed at realising and fulfilling Potential. The model can equally be applied to an individual, a team or a business.

The Dynamics of Potential consists of four key parts – The Four Ps – each part important in its own right yet integral to the whole to ensure ongoing success and fulfilment. The book follows and explores the individual parts of the model, providing insight, personal reflections and learnings, self-development tools and exercises.

Perspective

In the Perspective section we ask some searching questions to help you gain insight: How well do you know yourself? Are you aware of your strengths and are you using them to your advantage and to maximise your own and your team's performance? Are you allowing self-limiting beliefs to restrict opportunities and the potential that lies within you?

By gaining a clearer perspective of yourself and others, you can create a solid foundation to define your purpose effectively and articulate who you are, where you are now and where you aspire to go.

Purpose

We then move on to look at defining a Purpose. Do you have a clear sense of purpose, of what you want to achieve and what's important to you? Have you defined personal values that can shape and influence your decisions? Have you visualised your future, devised a plan and know how to implement it? How will you review progress and keep motivated?

Having a sense of purpose is fundamental to achieving your potential and getting what you want out of life, both personally and professionally.

Performance

To achieve your Potential you need to improve your Performance. Are you getting the best out of yourself, your team and your business? What areas of your performance require support and increased focus? How can you continually improve performance to create further opportunities?

Enhancing your performance and that of the team will lead to the business becoming stronger and create new opportunities for you and all those associated with its success.

Progress

Finally, we look at continuing to Progress. Are you clear of your next steps? Are you in a position of influence and strength to take control of your development and future? How do you create a learning culture to support others towards their personal goals?

Progress is essential to the success of you, your team and the business. Embrace change and continually strive to grow and develop to maximise your potential and be ready for the next challenge.

For the Four Ps of Potential to be effectively realised I have identified three **critical success factors** that will prove fundamental to successful implementation. They are each important yet can be life changing and potentially transform the performance of your team and business if they are consistently applied in equal measure. These critical success factors of **Positivity, Balance and Environment** are regular themes throughout the book and are key to each part of the model. Most importantly, you are in control and can influence all three of them.

Positivity

A positive frame of mind encourages a can-do attitude in yourself and others. Positivity motivates, influences and breeds success. You can choose to be either drained and demotivated by always looking at the downsides and what hasn't gone right, or be energised and upbeat by the positives and the opportunities. **Inspirational leaders and managers look up and look forward,** and draw on their positive mindset to encourage and motivate themselves and others to success.

Balance

Adopting a balanced approach in your personal and professional life creates a strong foundation from which to take decisive, effective and consistent action. Balance provides you with stability and influences a more inclusive and rounded approach.

In business, balance is essential. The best performing businesses recognise the importance of a balanced approach for maximising profitability through developing and investing in their people and delivering high service standards to their customers in equal measure. Just focusing on cutting costs at the expense of their people and customers creates a long-term negative imbalance.

Environment

Working environments and company cultures can be very different. Creating success and fulfilling your own potential and that of others can be dependent on the culture being conducive to your values, your thinking and your preferred working style. Some professional cultures can stifle you and make you question your own potential and value, while others can be energising, supportive and rewarding.

Find a culture and environment that's right for you or one you can positively influence and make a difference to, in order to maximise your potential and the potential of others.

Use the **Dynamics of Potential** business model to support your thinking, performance and continual development so you can understand and then achieve your aspirations.

PART ONE: Perspective

Know your strengths and discover your untapped potential

CHAPTER 1

Discover and embrace your strengths

"Each person's greatest room for growth lies in the
areas of his or her greatest strength."
Buckingham and Clifton, *Now, Discover Your Strengths*

When it comes to developing your potential it's not enough to focus on improving your weaknesses. Maximum impact can be gained by leveraging your strengths.

When you're thinking about your potential and developing it, there is a tendency to focus on what's not going well or on your limitations. However, there is more to be gained by focusing on and identifying your strengths, and making them stronger.

Focusing on areas of non-performance and weakness can diminish resources, drain energy and reduce motivation, whereas if you focus on strength, it motivates, inspires, creates energy and excitement. The impact that it has can be significant. Buckingham and Clifton, in their book *Now, Discover Your Strengths*, argue that by focusing on identifying, practising and refining your strengths, you become more productive, more fulfilled and more successful in the things that matter most.

By accepting that we are all different, have different strengths, and that weaknesses are part of everyone's character, we grow and develop. Think about it: how realistic is it to turn every weakness you have into a strength? Is it even possible? If you focus on your strengths – what works for you, what motivates you, what inspires you – you'll be coming from a more positive approach. Focus on what you're good at and what you can do, rather than what doesn't work and what you're not so good at.

FIND IT! Build on strengths

Whenever I appointed someone into a new role, I always gave them one piece of advice to support them: focus on what's right and not on what's going wrong. Identify and build on the strengths and successes.

A newly appointed General Manger would often list their issues and concerns, highlighting problems that needed to be dealt with and emphasising the amount of time and energy required to put things right. The extent of the list sometimes overwhelmed them, drained their energy and motivation, and occasionally was used to create the impression, rightly or wrongly, that there was so much to do.

By adopting a different approach, by focusing on the positives within the business and identifying the successes, we can create a position of strength from which to tackle some of the issues and weaknesses. It's more energising, motivational, and liberating.

It is crucial in any new role to step back, watch and learn; list all your first impressions, but don't let the strengths and positives of the business be clouded by the tendency to focus on the problems and weaknesses and what is wrong.

Identify and build on the strengths to help you to overcome some of the weaknesses.

Your Personal Strengths

So, what are your strengths? How do you define them and improve them? Alex Linley, the founder of the Center of Applied Positive Psychology (CAPP) which focuses on spreading the word about strengths and their role in the field of positive psychology, says that a strength is a capacity that already exists within us. It is something that comes naturally. Using a strength feels authentic; it's energising. Weaknesses, in contrast, often drain us.

When you stop focusing on your weaknesses and start playing to your strengths, you can transform your life. Most people are very good at identifying their flaws: "Oh, I'm not good at this. This isn't my strength."

If we turn that around and say, "I'm great at this and my strengths include..." the mindset changes.

Strengths will vary between individuals and can be both behavioural and task orientated. Typical strengths could include:

- Being well-planned, organised and disciplined
- Communicating in a natural and confident manner
- Analysing and interpreting data
- Having empathy with others
- Motivating and encouraging others
- Completing tasks
- Influencing others
- Having resilience and an inner strength
- Being focused and determined.

You may not be aware of your own personal strengths. You may be aware of some but have conditioned your thinking to exclude or limit others. If you are not fully aware of your personal strengths you might not utilise them, and as a result limit the potential within you, so miss out on greater opportunity both personally and professionally.

Before you can build on your strengths, you have to identify them.

Steps to discover your own personal strengths:

Articulate your personal strengths by making a list. What qualities do you see in yourself? When you believe you can find no more, challenge yourself to find another five. List a minimum of ten strengths and reflect upon and acknowledge each one.

Ask others. Ask people, both inside and outside of work, who know you well and whose judgement you respect and trust. Some of their answers may not have been included in your initial list.

Learn from others. What strengths do you admire in others? Perhaps you have a role model or a mentor. Look at their strengths and then think about whether you demonstrate any of those strengths yourself.

Focus on the activities that you enjoy and that bring you the most satisfaction. What strengths are you using that come naturally?

Notice what you do differently to everyone else. In a situation where you are truly using your strengths you will stand out from a crowd. Your approach will be unique. To name your strengths, you want to identify those moments and note how you are different.

Figure out what comes naturally to you. Break these strengths down to identify what skills you are using.

Work with a coach. A strengths-based coaching approach will support you to articulate your strengths clearly and build upon them.

Go online and take a **strengths assessment** (see below).

Strengths Assessment

The most widely recognised online Strengths Assessments are the following:

Gallup Strength Finder – through research, a list of thirty-four personal strengths have been identified against which an individual is measured. The entry level assessment is the first step in helping you identify your strengths and talents and highlights your top five strengths out of the thirty-four A comprehensive report is produced of your top five strengths and what makes you stand out. Recommendations and useful insights are detailed on how to start utilising your strengths to gain maximum advantage. Entry level requires a minimal charge.

Values in Action (VIA) – core character strengths based around twenty-four personal values. An entry level report, which is free, ranks your top twenty-four strengths in order. This is more of a holistic approach focusing on your values and what they mean to you, and how they can help you lead a happier, more engaging and satisfying life. There are more detailed reports, analysis and recommendations which can be purchased for an affordable cost.

CAPP R2 Strengths Profiler – measures sixty attributes across three dimensions of performance, energy and use. Results are grouped into four areas covering: Realised Strengths – things you find energising, perform well and use often; Unrealised Strengths – things you find energising and perform well but don't use so often; Learnt Behaviours – things you have learnt to do well, but that don't energise you; and Weaknesses – things you find hard to do well and find draining. Entry level is comprehensive with a set of helpful and insightful reports at an affordable cost.

Whatever method you use to identify your strengths will bring you one step closer to improving them.

What are your greatest strengths?

Having interviewed many potential employees over my career, I consistently ask one question: "What are your greatest strengths?" The answer to this question can tell me a great deal about the individual. Answers range from the candidate struggling to identify anything of significance to an exhaustive list of attributes plucked directly from a leadership book, telling me what they think I want to hear.

If you ever get asked that question be prepared and articulate your response with genuine authenticity. Some of the best responses include:

Highlighting several identified strengths and then prioritising the strongest. *"My key strengths lie with getting the best out of people, in particular giving honest and constructive feedback to allow my team to improve their performance."*

Tailoring the strength to the relevance of the opportunity or individual. *"In a sales environment it is most important to develop a chemistry and affinity with your client, and this is a strength that now comes naturally to me."*

Giving examples of how that strength has been used to the maximum. *"One of my greatest strengths lies in building relationships with others, so I have put myself forward to represent the company at networking events."*

Demonstrating what you have done to build on that area of strength. *"I am really interested in understanding my strengths and how to make them stronger so I decided to carry out an online exercise. It highlighted strengths such as communication and organisational skills which I hadn't recognised in myself, but I am now more conscious of these and how I utilise them in my job effectively."*

Showing how you could use that strength going forward. *"Coaching my team to deliver the best service they can is something that I enjoy and consider to be one of my strengths. I have now been asked to apply my knowledge to other departments to support their teams."*

Strengths at work

A strengths-based approach to managing teams can also benefit businesses. Marcus Buckingham effectively highlights the importance of a strengths-based approach within your business. His findings demonstrate that great companies must not only recognise that each employee is different, but they must capitalise on these differences. He states that the employers must watch for clues to each employee's natural talents and then develop these talents into bona fide strengths.

Build strengths from personal to team to business

Your strengths are brought into play when you work alone, or in a team or as part of the business. You may use different strengths as you find yourself in different roles in the business or your career. When a business is able to see a person's strengths and find ways to use them effectively, this will have a positive bottom line impact. Often leaders and managers use the appraisal system and strengths profiling to identify the strengths they have within their team members.

Think about your last appraisal or performance review. How much time and focus did you spend looking at your strengths and the positives? How much time did you spend focusing on areas of development and weaknesses? Think about what you did as a result of that appraisal. How much time did you spend on leveraging your strengths and making them stronger?

Invariably, more time is spent focusing and discussing the weaker areas as opposed to getting more from the strengths team members have. This goes across the team and business reviews too, where often the stronger or well-performing parts of the business are bypassed, and the weak parts are identified as the key areas for development and improvement.

Work it! Get more from your high performers

As part of a central Executive Team, we met regularly to review the performance of each hotel within the group. Most of our time was spent focusing on the poor performing hotels and discussing what actions could be taken to improve their results. We would divert and direct resources to a hotel to readdress and support an issue or problem that was impacting the performance of the business. On reflection, very little time was spent discussing the high performers –what we could we learn from them and what support we could offer to make them even better.

We could, perhaps, have better utilised specialist and expert resources to get more out of the successes and strengths within the performing business as well as putting out fires and restoring normality in the under-performing hotels.

Use your strengths to get more out of the high performers, which can add more value to the overall business. We successfully adopted this approach when setting profit targets per hotel to reach an overall company target. We asked more from the hotels that were performing well as there was more opportunity to maximise and grow the business from a position of strength.

Play to your strengths and get more from your high performers.

When an organisation plays to the strengths of its team, it can create stronger business units by:

- Putting people together who complement each other's strengths and cover the weaknesses
- Creating reverse mentoring schemes: putting less experienced people with the more experienced, so both can develop.

A recent Gallup survey (http://www.gallup.com – survey conducted in the USA in 2014) found that organisations focusing on maximising the natural talents of their employees increase engagement levels by an average of 33% per year. Only about one in three employees strongly agrees that they've had an opportunity to do what they do best every day. In the survey, for the 37% who agreed that their supervisor focused on their strengths, active disengagement fell dramatically to 1%. This suggests that if all companies train their managers to focus on employees' strengths, they could double the number of engaged employees in the workplace.

More than half (52%) of the respondents who use their strengths for three hours a day or fewer are stressed, but this falls to 36% for those who use their strengths ten hours per day or more. Gallup's data show that simply by learning their strengths, companies make employees 7.8% more productive, and teams that focus on strengths every day have 12.5% greater productivity.

Gallup has found that building employees' strengths is a far more effective approach to improving performance than working on weaknesses. When employees know and use their strengths, they are more engaged, perform better, and are less likely to leave the company.

Own it! Are you playing to your strengths?

It is not unusual that, as you grow within a business and take up more responsibilities, you continually face many new challenges that sometimes don't play to your strengths or skill set. You may also find that you become less motivated or less energised. When I reflect on my career in hospitality, the highlights for me were all about people: developing, building and leading great teams of people and sharing their passion for delivering excellent levels of service to the customer; being in the business at the sharp end and getting a buzz from the shop floor.

As my career developed and I became CEO and a member of the Board, my remit was very different. My role pulled me further away from what I really enjoyed and more towards high level meetings with the bank, potential investors and the Board. Much of my time was spent locked away in my office, planning and preparing for the various meetings, and then in board rooms presenting and debating various strategic issues, largely finance related. While I found this part of my role challenging, interesting and an opportunity to broaden my knowledge and deepen my understanding, I also found it quite draining and de-energising and it wasn't motivating me in the same way.

Sometimes you have to listen to yourself and understand where your strengths lie and how you are using them to give you energy, purpose and motivation in what you do.

Talents become strengths

If you want to be a great leader, consider these two assumptions:

- Each person's talents are enduring and unique
- Each person's greatest room for growth is in the areas of his or her greatest strength.

A talent could be untapped, or something that you use in other areas of your life but perhaps don't realise you could use in a work context, or even what others see in you that you don't see. **For that talent to become a strength you have to grow it, use it, build it, like a muscle.**

With the above two assumptions in mind, use these four steps to build a strength based business:

1 Spend a great deal of time and money to select the right people in the first place
2 Focus on performance rather than legislating outcomes. Don't describe each step; allow people to find their way using their strengths

3 Invest time and resources into learning about an individual's strengths and figuring out how to build on these strengths, rather than plugging the "skills gap"

4 Devise ways to help each person grow their career without necessarily promoting them up the corporate ladder and out of their areas of strength.

I have seen many examples, when I have been coaching, of individuals who have grown within their businesses, but as a result have not played to their strengths. Here are just a couple:

A talented sales person has been promoted and is now leading a sales team; she has become more of a people manager than a sales person. Her strength is doing business and sealing deals in front of the customer, but she has now been taken away from the customer and is spending most of her time managing, leading and reviewing teams. She's become more internal than external and not playing to her strengths. She's not as motivated by what she's doing.

I have also coached a marketing specialist who now does very little marketing as he is managing the marketing team and spends more time presenting, communicating and influencing up the line. This supports the findings of the survey, concluding that the longer an employee stays with a business and the higher they climb the traditional career ladder, the less likely they are to be playing to their strengths.

The challenge is whether the individual can adapt, build and develop new strengths to complement their existing ones.

Work it! Play to employees' strengths

I was fortunate to work alongside a very talented Hotel General Manager whose passion was to surprise and delight his guests by his commitment to the quality of his product and the service that his team delivered. He was always highly visible to both his team and his guests, and his eye for quality was exceptional. His hotel was a centre of excellence within the company.

He was then promoted to a central role with responsibility for driving and enhancing quality across all the hotels within the company. Although the logic behind creating this role for him was a sound one and was based upon his area of strength, it sadly did not translate into success.

He found it difficult to influence from a central perspective and his skills for delivering and enhancing quality at one hotel through an individualised approach could not be translated into a wider remit. The skill set required to be successful in the role was very different and proved more challenging than focusing on one specialist area of strength. He returned to his role as General Manager and played to his strength once again, which also proved to be more motivational to him.

As an employee grows and gets promoted within the business, ensure that their key strengths are not lost in the transition.

Acknowledge your weakness – it's a strength

We all have weaknesses. Even great leaders and the most successful businesses have weaknesses. We have to recognise and acknowledge that we can't be good at everything – although many leaders feel they have to be. The challenge is to recognise and accept your weaknesses in the same way as you do with your strengths and then to take some form of action.

Much is written and talked about transforming a weakness into a strength. If we focus on a particular weakness with a positive and open mindset then anything is possible. However, I believe the energy and time spent can perhaps be disproportionate to the result.

Instead, focus on acknowledging your weaknesses and limit their impact on you and your business:

Admit and accept the weakness exists.

Effectively manage the weakness – spend more time and energy on developing and fine tuning your strengths.

Be in control – avoid putting yourself in situations where your weakness may be highlighted.

Get good enough – a weakness doesn't have to become a strength, but place importance on learning, practising and achieving enough to get by.

Use the strengths of others to support you – delegate and empower others to complement your strengths.

Be prepared - take time and preparation to deal with your weakness. Excellent preparation can make up for a lot and give you more confidence.

Summary

If you focus on the positive - on what you're good at, on your strengths - it drives motivation, energising you rather than draining your energy. I have a tendency to focus on my weaknesses and have to make an effort to remember my own strengths, When I do this, I feel more motivated, energised and positive.

We all have more strengths than we may realise.

"Only when you operate from strengths can you achieve true excellence. You must develop a thorough understanding of your strengths and weaknesses, and discover where you can make the biggest contribution to your organisation."
Peter Drucker, Management Consultant

CHAPTER 2

Don't let your thinking limit your potential

"It's not what you don't know that holds you back;
it's what you do know that isn't true."
Jack Canfield, Author

Most of us are better and capable of more than we think we are, but only if we believe it. Believing in yourself is a choice, a choice that you make every day. If you are aiming to be successful in both your personal and professional life, you have to take responsibility and believe that you are capable of making your goals happen. Many of us may not fulfil our own potential nor try new experiences simply because we don't perceive ourselves as capable of doing so.

Your thinking impacts your Potential

If you shy away from putting yourself forward for a new job or resist taking on more responsibility to grow and develop, the problem may not be the situation but your own perception, your own thinking. How you think about yourself can determine how successful you can be. Don't let your thinking limit your potential, as I nearly did.

Own it! Don't limit yourself

I can remember it very clearly. I had been a General Manager within the Forte Posthouse division for fewer than four years when a vacancy was circulated to become a Regional Director within the Heritage Collection with responsibility for over twenty hotels. I read the vacancy and then put it in the bin. I never thought for a moment that I would be the person appointed to that role – a role that transformed my career.

My initial reaction was that I wasn't capable – I didn't have the experience, I wouldn't have the confidence and there were far stronger candidates than me. This was a classic case of allowing my inner voice to focus on all the reasons why I would not consider myself worthy of applying for the position. My thinking was limiting my future potential and success.

If it hadn't been for my boss at the time, who had an eye for discovering and encouraging potential leaders, there was no way that I would have put myself forward for the role. I have a lot to thank him for. He highlighted to me all the reasons why he considered me to be a strong candidate and made me reflect, consider and discard many of the negative thoughts that were holding me back.

Don't let your thinking stand in the way of a great opportunity. Talk yourself up, not down. Believe in yourself.

What are limiting assumptions?

Everyone is capable of more if **they** believe they are. I have been fortunate to be able to fulfil my potential in the hospitality sector due to making the most of the opportunities that I have been given, but I see many people around me who have become frustrated because they haven't yet fulfilled theirs or had the confidence and belief to do so.

I recently took a call from an ex-colleague who asked for my opinion about accepting a job that she had been offered. She'd gone through a rigorous interview process against other great candidates and was successful in her application, yet she was asking me whether I felt she was capable. While she had interviewed well, demonstrating confidence and capability in the process, in her own mind she had doubts about whether she would be successful at the job. She lacked confidence, and already her worries and fears were overwhelming her. Others saw more in her than she was able to recognise or acknowledge in herself, and due to her lack of self-belief she almost walked away from the opportunity. She has since thrived in the new role and displays a high level of confidence even though her inner voice is still doubting her.

We talk more about this feeling, the imposter syndrome, in Chapter 7.

Often when people lack confidence the problem is not the actual situation, but more their perception of themselves and their beliefs about their capabilities. How you think about yourself can determine how successful you can be, so don't let your thinking limit your potential nor close your mind. Challenge your thinking and listen to others. They may see something that you haven't, or may see the situation from a different angle.

Your thinking can not only limit yourself, but you can also limit others if you don't have more of an open approach.

Work it! Keep an open mind

A trusted and well-respected colleague of mine put forward a candidate for a General Manager vacancy to me for consideration. I was not convinced of the calibre of the candidate nor whether he would be able to rise to the challenge of this particular hotel. I had known him for some years and had a lot of time and respect for him, but following recent meetings with him I felt he lacked self-confidence and the ability to drive and inspire a team.

Despite my concerns, which I raised with my colleague, I gave my support to the appointment.

He very quickly made a positive impact on the business, turned out to be one of our best performing General Managers, and was promoted within the business to take on senior management positions. On reflection, I realised that my earlier assumptions about him had restricted my ability to see all his qualities and that my thinking could have limited his potential and opportunity within the business. My initial thoughts about his potential were misplaced, and I was thankful that I'd listened to my colleague who'd had the confidence to make and support the appointment.

Keep an open mind and listen, especially when your initial reaction and thoughts may cloud your judgement on others.

Breaking barriers: the four minute mile

The inspirational story of Roger Bannister has always resonated with me, and I used it during my opening address at a company annual conference to challenge ways of thinking. Roger Bannister is significant not only for his personal achievement, planning, hard work and determination in being the first athlete to break the four-minute mile, but also for what happened next. Plenty of people had said that it was impossible to run a mile in under four minutes; doctors even believed that a human was physically incapable of doing so. Within months of Roger Bannister breaking the four-minute mile, however, many other runners had also managed it. Once that barrier, that limit, had been removed, others were more readily able to achieve it too.

What had been holding them back?

The story implies that belief alone explains why other runners followed suit so quickly. If we think about this in the business terms of achieving or exceeding a target, we can see how once we have broken a limit– by belief, hard work and determination – we pave the way for others to follow. I challenged the business to learn from the Roger Bannister story and to apply the learnings to a business opportunity to improve performance.

The focus for the company that year was to achieve higher average room rates in line with the recent bedroom refurbishments. The targets that had been set were far higher than anyone had imagined and were considered by many to be unrealistic and unachievable.

As a result, we examined our approach, reviewed our strategy and, more importantly, we challenged our thinking and our belief. What was preventing us from charging the rate and achieving the target? When it came to it, it was really only ourselves and our limiting assumptions that were holding us back. Within a few months of really focusing on that target, one hotel smashed the barrier, and after that a number of hotels quickly followed.

Own it! "Think big"

Achieving budgets and targets are fundamental to the success of a business. Throughout my career success has been dependant on whether financial budgets and targets have been achieved. However, I have experienced many different approaches to the budgeting process.

One company I worked for had a very aspirational approach to budgeting and targeting with the strategy of setting exceptionally high targets, which resulted in a consensus that they were unachievable and unrealistic. The rationale behind the approach, however, is sound. "Think big". Stretch and challenge your mind, your team, your business to think differently to achieve more. If you set a budget to improve your profitability by 30%, you may achieve 20%. If it is set at a realistic 8%, you may exceed it by just 2% and be satisfied.

I adopted this approach to a charity that I was a trustee for. The fundraising target was modest and every year grew incrementally by a minimal percentage. Targets were invariably met, although they weren't greatly exceeded. Despite an initial resistance to a significantly increased fundraising target, people swiftly focused their minds on new initiatives. Their existing thought processes and how things had been done were challenged, and gradually the mood became more energised and forward thinking. They achieved and exceeded the unrealistic target.

By having an aspirational target and "thinking big" you can achieve more if you put your positive mind to it. Don't let your limiting beliefs stifle performance.

How do self-limiting assumptions occur?

We are all born into this world with no sense of what we can or cannot achieve, but as we grow we start to teach ourselves to set limits and cap our expectations. Our assumptions are influenced and controlled by our beliefs.

Beliefs are not facts and are invariably built on nothing more than deeply ingrained memories or interpretations of our experiences over time. The more that we think these thoughts, the more we believe them; they are reinforced, ingrained and become the "norm". They gradually become commands and influencers to our nervous system that shape, filter and generalise our thoughts.

As our life evolves and our careers and opportunities develop and change, our beliefs tend to remain constant, and can sometimes hold us back, **pulling us back from pushing ourselves forward.**

Here are some examples of beliefs that could be holding you back:

"I made a mistake, so I will always make this mistake." This all-or-nothing mentality lends itself to self-limiting assumptions. We are good at dwelling on our mistakes.

"I'm not good at this yet, so I never will be." This belief often occurs when we're trying something new, when we are a novice. Our first attempt leads to mistakes, so our belief builds from our novice position. Failure and learning from it is how we get better.

"They didn't like my proposal, so no one will like my proposals." It's easier to focus on the negative. This self-limiting assumption is a generalisation and can drain our confidence to try again.

"No one's ever complained, so I must be good." A lack of complaints doesn't prove talent. Don't become complacent nor let your ego drive you.

Find it! Step back to move forwards

When you are immersed in your business it is sometimes challenging to recognise and appreciate the progress that you have made. When setbacks occur and problems arise, which they will, there can be a tendency to generalise and allow your thinking to focus on what's not been achieved rather than what has. If that thought pattern continues, the negative thinking can become stronger and more distorted.

I encourage individuals who struggle to see the good from the bad to think back to the day they started their new job or a new position and then articulate all the progress they have achieved within the business.

It is only when you step back and reflect that your progress becomes clearer and more reflective of reality.

Memories form our beliefs. There are plenty of researchers who have explored the workings of the brain and how memories are made. The work of Jenny Rogers (http://jennyrogerscoaching.com) is interesting, and a great place to continue your own reading. Some key points:

Neuroscientific research shows that emotions drive human behaviour and thinking. This creates a preference in the human brain to stick with what it knows and has done before.

Our limbic system is the emotional centre of the brain, responsible for our learning and memory. The amygdala is part of the limbic system and is the brain's "alarm system", storing memories of previous situations which have aroused strong negative emotion, resisting rational analysis and reducing our ability to think properly in stressful situations.

When we're faced with anything outside of our comfort zone that we perceive as difficult, fearful or challenging, the amygdala sends the stress hormone cortisol to close down the more logical part of the brain: the pre-frontal cortex. The pre-frontal cortex controls our reasoning, communication, planning and moral awareness. It focuses on the positives and can generate optimism. We need to bring the pre-frontal cortex into prominence consciously as it can release neurotransmitters that calm down the amygdala.

There's a great book, *The Chimp Paradox*, by Professor Steve Peters, which explains the struggles going on in our minds. He simplifies the science, offering a metaphor for the amygdala of the chimp mind that needs to be understood, controlled and managed, to allow the brain's executive function (pre-frontal cortex) to have more influence over our thinking and emotions.

How to overcome self-limiting assumptions

How do you recognise your self-limiting assumptions? Jack Canfield, a leading coach and author of *The Success Principles*, explains that if you are going to be successful you need to give up the phrases "I can't" and "I wish I was able". These phrases disempower you and make you weaker when you say them. To fulfil your potential, it is important to remove the limitations you may be putting on yourself.

Step back and review what you have already achieved – don't focus too much on the challenges that lie ahead which cause a sense of anxiety or discouragement. It is easy to get so wrapped up in what we don't have and haven't accomplished that we don't often realise what we do have. It's easy to feel like we're not doing as well as we should, but sometimes we have to pay attention and measure our progress more objectively.

Give yourself credit for what you've achieved – celebrate your successes, acknowledge them and take confidence from them. Don't pay lip service to your achievements, bring them to the forefront of your mind and use them to reinforce your positive outlook.

Listen to others – be receptive to positive feedback and encouragement from others. Really listen, embrace what is being said and believe it. Don't use your personal filter to hear only what you want to hear and what you think you believe.

Monitor your own progress – not the progress that others make. Compare yourself to how you were yesterday or last week. Take confidence from how **you** are progressing as opposed to someone else who may be progressing faster.

Create a "can-do" mindset – develop your thinking to see the positives in every situation. If you develop your mindset to believe that setbacks and weaknesses aren't really what you perceive them to be, you'll have broken through your limitations and fears.

Re-examine and discard the limiting ideas you have about yourself.

Face your fears

With my coaching clients, I use the acronym of FEAR: False Evidence Appearing Real.

In our minds we create an assumption, we dwell on this false evidence and it then appears real to us. In reality, what we fear is not happening, but we believe that it is, and that fear then prevents us from doing things, from taking action. The FEAR stands in the way of something we want to achieve. Almost all our fears are self-created, but they can be challenged and overcome.

Of course, feeling fearful is natural. Everyone feels fear. It is a normal emotion just like anxiety or stress, but if it is not controlled or dealt with effectively, it can restrict and limit the potential you have within you.

If fear is so common and a natural emotion that prevents us from overcoming obstacles and challenges, how can we ever reach our potential? I believe it is more about our ability to deal with and control the fear as opposed to eliminating it.

Here are four steps to help you deal with your fears:

- Acknowledge and embrace the fear
- Get behind the reasons for the fear and understand them
- Replace the emotion of fear with confidence and excitement
- Be prepared to accept that you might fail, but if you do then you can and will deal with it.

Practise positive self-talk

From early on in my career I have been a strong advocate of positive self-talk. It was first introduced to me during an early management programme that I attended, "The Pacific Institute", which was initiated by one of the most progressive and innovative HR Directors I have worked with, who went on to become a leading HR Director within the hospitality sector. She is now among the best leadership coaches that I have met, and I am fortunate that she is one of my mentors.

The management programme helped to shape my positive thinking. However, positive self-talk does not come naturally to me, and like all good disciplines it needs focus, energy and practise.

How you talk to yourself can be either empowering or harmful to reaching your potential. Your self-talk can either support you to success or limit your potential to succeed. How you decide to use your inner voice is within your control – you can positively use it to your advantage or you can allow it to hold you back. When you reflect on how you use it currently, why would you choose any other way than positively?

Positive self-talk is the simple process of influencing yourself to keep motivated, focused and confident. Talking yourself up rather than talking yourself down; focusing on the positives rather than negatives; encouraging rather than discouraging. As I've previously mentioned, the brain gives more attention to negative experiences than positive ones, so looking at the positives takes deliberate effort. However, you are in control. You have a choice. You can decide whether to be positive or negative, happy or sad, optimistic or pessimistic.

Barbara Fredrickson, a leading positive psychology researcher, reports that by focusing on positive emotions you will experience more possibilities in your life. She refers to this as the **"broaden and build"** theory because positive emotions broaden your sense of possibilities and open your mind, which in turn allows you to build new skills and resources that can provide value in other areas of your life.

How to encourage positive self-talk and tame your inner critic:

Develop awareness of your thoughts – just because you think it doesn't mean it is true or going to happen.

Challenge – many of our thoughts are exaggerated, generalised or biased.

Don't replay a negative experience – reframe it instead. What can you learn from it? Distract yourself away from thinking about it.

Worst case scenario – when your inner critic is being negative and it says you cannot do something and gives you that fear, take a moment to relax and ask yourself two questions. Really? Why? See if your inner critic has got an answer for you or whether it's just scared.

Give yourself an independent view – what advice would you give someone else?

Always search for and concentrate on the positive emotion – find a positive out of a negative.

Find it! Practise positive self-talk

I was less than a year into my new coaching business, and despite having gained some clients I had been unsuccessful in a couple of pitches. I found myself generalising about my ability to win clients and whether this new career was right for me. I would reflect too heavily on the reasons as to why I didn't gain the business and focus all the attention on me, as opposed to acknowledging the many other reasons that influenced the decision – the majority of which were outside of my control.

I had to work hard at keeping my inner critic at bay – which I did, and I continue to do so. Coaching encourages you to think differently and challenge your thinking. I spent time focusing on and acknowledging my achievements to date – the contracts that I had won; the clients who had renewed and extended their assignment with me; the potential clients I had made through networking; the significant impact that I was already having for my clients. I had achieved so much in such a short space of time – I just needed to remind myself of the facts.

Positive self-talk doesn't come naturally to everyone and you will find even the most confident of people will be struggling at times with their inner critic. Practise using it and it will develop and come more naturally over time.

Maintain a balanced approach

As with all things, finding a balance is necessary. Achieving positive self-talk and confidence rather than becoming over-confident and arrogant can be a challenge for some people. Perception is reality, and no matter how good your intentions are, what is of most importance is how you are perceived. There's a fine line between confidence and arrogance. Where confidence is motivational, inspiring and positive, arrogance has the reverse impact on others. If you tend to be over-confident and believe you are capable of anything, you will need to find a balanced approach when managing your ego so that your over-confidence is not interpreted as arrogance.

Summary

Don't let your limiting beliefs and fears hold you back or limit your potential. Identify and acknowledge them and make positive steps to change the way you deal with and manage them. You are in control of what you are saying to yourself and how you choose to react.

"Believe you can and you're halfway there."
Theodore Roosevelt

CHAPTER 3

Know where you are and acknowledge your success so you can go even further

"Until you make the unconscious conscious, it will direct your life and you will call it fate."

CG Jung

Self-awareness allows you to be more empowered to make changes, build on your areas of strength and tackle those self-limiting beliefs. It supports you to understand who you are, where you are, and influences you to recognise what you have achieved.

In simple terms, self-awareness is about getting to know yourself and then getting to know yourself even better. It's about learning to understand why you feel what you feel and why you behave how you behave. Once you begin to understand yourself better you will then have the freedom and opportunity to change things about yourself and create a life and a career that you want. Having clarity about who you are and what you want out of your personal and professional life can be empowering, giving you the confidence to influence and make changes.

The importance of being self-aware

Self-awareness is one of the key areas focused on in coaching. A role of the coach is to increase your self-awareness so that you can take responsibility for your behaviour, your emotions, what you have achieved and what you want to do going forward.

When you're coaching yourself or others, being self-aware will make all the difference. Self-awareness encourages you to act consciously rather than passively, and in turn that will help you have a more positive outlook on life.

When you become self-aware you are able to identify areas where you would like to make changes and improvements. Self-awareness helps you to react to situations in the way that you want to, positively impacting your behaviour rather than automatically responding in a reactive and uncontrolled manner. If you condition your mind to react in a certain way, then when you encounter a similar event in the future, you are better able to respond. Self-awareness allows you to be conscious of conditioning and preconceptions, and can form the foundation of freeing and opening the mind.

An executive leadership study, "What Predicts Executive Success" by organisational consulting firm Green Peak Partners in collaboration with a research team at Cornell University, explains the importance of self-awareness in leadership. The study shows that "results-at-all-costs" executives actually diminish the bottom line, while self-aware leaders with strong interpersonal skills deliver better financial performance. A high self-awareness score is the strongest predictor of overall success.

"Executives who are aware of their weaknesses are often better able to hire subordinates who perform well in areas in which the leader lacks acumen," said Dr Winkler, Principal at Green Peak Partners.

The research demonstrates that self-aware leaders, who understand themselves and can relate to others, are generally more successful. Many people believe that leaders who are nice guys and display the soft skills at the expense of a more ruthless approach finish last, but research shows nice guys can finish first.

The soft skills create success.

Own it! Nice guys finish first

The findings of the study conducted by Green Peak Partners resonated with me. I have often been perceived as a "nice guy" and been told that my more inclusive, consultative and supportive leadership style doesn't deliver results as effectively as being tough, harsh and uncompromising. While trying to remain authentic in my leadership approach and through consciously developing my own self-awareness, which I have found quite challenging, I have felt more confident in myself to be who I am and not what others want me to be.

Managers and leaders come in all shapes and sizes with differing approaches and styles. By becoming more aware of your own strengths, weaknesses, behaviours and management approach, you can develop and enhance your own style to maximum advantage.

You can be a "nice person" and still be an effective and successful leader. Be more aware of what makes you the leader you are and have confidence to embrace those qualities.

Why it's a challenge to be self-aware

We don't always see what others see, so when we get frank feedback from them we are often surprised. Most of the time we simply do not observe ourselves; it takes a conscious effort and we largely operate on automatic pilot, unconscious of what we are doing or how we are feeling. We may find it difficult to focus on the here and now as our minds have a tendency to wander. We can address this problem with the mindfulness exercises found in "Chapter 7: Be the best you can".

From "Chapter 2: Don't let your thinking limit your potential", we learnt that our minds tend to see some form of bias, be that positive or negative, that impacts our ability to have an accurate understanding of ourselves. Frequently we focus on what we don't do well as opposed to what we do right.

How to increase your self-awareness to leverage the benefits

It is sometimes a challenge to know where you really are, and then even more of a challenge to identify where you can go from there. We are naturally biased towards our own opinions and behaviours.

So, what can you do to improve your self-awareness? These are a few assessment exercises that can help.

Reflected Best Self

This evidence based tool is one of the most effective available and originated from research conducted at the University of Michigan. The basic principles and steps are:

Gather feedback and reflection from friends, colleagues and family about when they saw you at your best. Look for a good cross-section of your associates to get the best picture.

Look for patterns in their feedback. These patterns will help you identify your strengths.

Build your strengths profile from the patterns.

Take action. Prepare an action plan to build on your strengths.

The Professional Assessment Wheel

Sometimes called the Wheel of Life, the Professional Assessment Wheel is a simple yet powerful tool to support self-evaluation. It helps to identify your current situation with a view to raising awareness and gaining increased focus regarding areas of opportunity going forward, or gaps or shortfalls. It can be used from a personal or professional perspective or a combination of both. The wheel provides an opportunity for you to see the balance in what's important to you.

The simplest way to use the wheel is to choose the areas you want to focus on, plot them on the wheel, then rate yourself from one to ten on each of the spokes. Common themes for the spokes include job satisfaction, environment at work, relationships, health, family, salary, work/life balance, responsibility, etc. The website Coactive.com has a good example of this wheel.

This self-evaluation should support you to:

- Reflect on what you have done and where you are currently
- Think about what you might do next
- Consider your own progress and development.

It is only when you are clear about where you are now that you can work towards where you want to go in the future.

The Johari Window

This tool can be used on both an individual and team basis, providing you with the opportunity to understand how you and others see you and allowing you to focus on the areas in which you want to become more dominant. The Johari Window shows you four basic forms of self:

The Known or Public Self – the part of yourself that is visible for all to see. It reflects what you know about yourself and what others know about you.

The Blind Self – these are things that others know or see about you but you do not see yourself.

The Hidden or Private Self – what you see in yourself that is hidden and not recognised by others.

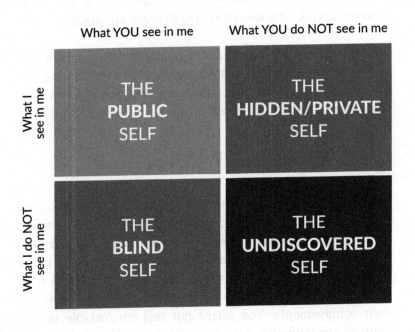

The Undiscovered Self – the things which neither you nor other people see.

If you want to know more about the Johari Window, you can research it and try it out here: http://kevan.org/johari. The process is straightforward and easy to implement: review a number of adjectives, and out of the long list select the six that you believe embody your character. Then invite others to select the six that they think best describe you. Putting the responses together generates your own personalised Johari Window.

The Johari Window helps people learn who they are with the help of other people's perceptions of them. When they are shared, these windows build knowledge, understanding and trust between people who are just getting to know one another.

Choose whichever tool you like to help you develop more self-awareness. **It's not about an individual tool, it's about finding that self-awareness and focusing on the outcome.** It's about creating space for yourself to give yourself time to really reflect.

Success breeds success

To allow yourself to know where you are and where you are heading it is important to recognise what you have achieved so far. Articulating your successes and achievements can be a challenging exercise for some, but it is important to do so. I have coached many clients who are senior and successful in their businesses, yet they struggle to demonstrate and acknowledge their achievements. You might not feel comfortable talking yourself up (although many people do, and sometimes talk themselves up more than they deserve), or you might not give yourself the space and time to reflect on and recollect your successes fully.

Success is relative and can mean different things to different people. It can be emotional as well as materialistic; it can be personal to you or through others. Success may be a promotion that you have earnt or seeing others you've coached and managed advance within the business. It is just as important to recognise the successes of others and their achievements within the business as it is to recognise your own.

Work it! Celebrate success

Success in business can be quite hard to articulate as it is not particularly tangible. Every business will have key achievements, but the nature of business is cyclical, and if you have a record year it soon gets forgotten when you start the new budget year with more demanding targets and higher expectations from your stakeholders.

I have always worked in companies that have placed great importance on a results-focused environment where sustaining peak performance was key to continually delivering expectations. I quickly realised the importance of acknowledging, sharing and celebrating success – creating a balanced approach between recognising past and current performance while pushing and encouraging future performance.

With my team, I introduced a culture of celebrating success across the business, the hotels and hotel departments. We held annual award ceremonies, recognised and rewarded monthly service champions, congratulated hotels that achieved their monthly budget, and the introduction of the "Hotel of the Month" award proved popular. These are just a few of our many initiatives that were positively received.

Recognising success and achievements throughout the business, no matter how small, has had a significant impact on the results of the business and the positive engagement from the team, providing a strong base from which to drive the business forward. Its success, however, depends on a consistent approach, as when achievements aren't recognised it can lead to a less engaged workforce.

Acknowledge and celebrate success before moving on to the next challenge. If achievements are dismissed and go unrecognised, the momentum and motivation to strive to be better decreases.

The more your successes and achievements are recognised, the more your self-esteem grows and the more confident you become in taking on and successfully achieving new projects and goals. List your successes then reinforce them – surprisingly, when you focus on them, you can recollect more than you initially realised.

Own it! Own your successes, acknowledge the success of others

There have been some people throughout my career who have claimed success at the expense of others, and some at my expense. Non-team players who placed more importance on "bigging themselves up" than the individuals on their teams who genuinely deserved the recognition and credit. These people tended to share the same egotistical yet insecure leadership traits, and not surprisingly struggled to encourage any team loyalty.

For you to become an inspirational and respected leader with a strong following, it is important to give the credit to whoever deserves it, and to admit to the part you played when something goes off track. The best leaders will also take personal responsibility for an issue on behalf of the team and then deal with and manage it later.

Take ownership of your own successes as well as standing up for your mistakes and misjudgements. Don't take personal credit at the expense of others as you will quickly damage your reputation and personal integrity.

However, as we know, our brain is wired to focus more on our failures and setbacks than on our successes. It has an ability to remember what we messed up, but is less inclined to remember what went well. This means we can underestimate and underappreciate the number of successes we have had.

Try this short exercise:

- Make a list of your successes
- Think about the emotions you felt when you achieved them, and make associations
- Reinforce the emotions by bringing the success back to the forefront of your mind
- Make this list visible; put it where you will see it every day.

Success builds confidence.
Confidence builds success.
Success builds success.

Find it! What are your gold medal moments?

I was presented with an opportunity to speak alongside the Olympic champion Alex Gregory at an event in London. Alex was part of the record-breaking rowing team which won gold at London and Rio in the coxless fours. The presentation topic was focused around sustaining peak performance with Alex drawing on his personal experiences and learnings from the world of sport while I applied some of my learnings and experiences from a business context.

I was aware that Alex would be bringing along his two gold medals to show to the audience which initially made me feel a little anxious about my own successes, especially in business where successes are invariably less tangible and impactful than in sport. He explained that his gold medals represented his immense achievements, his unwavering commitment and his sense of pride. They acted as a permanent recognition and reinforcement of his successes and achievements and a trigger for his associated emotions.

It got me thinking about success and influenced me to stop and reflect on my own achievements. Success is relative and will mean different things to different people. We all have successes, big and small, personal and professional, to be proud of and celebrate. However, not all of us will have a gold medal or an accolade to show for them and so they can be easily forgotten, pushed to the backs of our minds and mentally discarded. Don't lose sight of your gold medal moments – achievements and successes that mean something to you. Recognise them, embrace them, continually acknowledge them and find ways to tie them into your thinking to reinforce positive emotions. Success can significantly influence a positive mindset from which personal confidence can grow and lead to greater achievements.

I followed on from Alex's inspirational story of success and achievement and began my presentation with my gold medal moments – highlighting some of my professional and personal achievements and their significance to me. I then posed the following questions to the audience:

What are your gold medal moments?

What are the future gold medal moments that you are currently working towards?

It's too easy to lose sight of your successes and achievements and to think yourself less worthy than others. We all have achievements to be proud of. Recognise and embrace them.

Summary

Build self-awareness to get a better understanding and a more accurate picture of how you see yourself and how others see you. Identify and embrace your successes and take confidence from them to progress further and influence your future. When you know where you are you can then effectively plan where to go next.

In the next part of the book we will start looking at the How – how you can go further and the importance of having purpose, a plan and values to shape and influence the future. It's then all about taking action and making it happen.

"We know what we are,
but know not what we may be."
William Shakespeare

PART TWO: Purpose

Decide where you are heading and
make it happen

CHAPTER 4

The importance of purpose

> "Efforts and courage are not enough without purpose and direction."
> **John F Kennedy**

Why is having a purpose important?

Having a strong sense of purpose is fundamental to achieving your potential and getting what you want out of life. It keeps you driven and focused, and when combined with your own values, it can have a powerful impact on achieving your personal and professional goals.

Having purpose is like having a personal mission statement: you will know what you want to achieve and why. Once you've established a goal, the progress you make towards it gives you a sense of achievement and satisfaction, which can enhance your self-confidence and personal motivation. It can give you hope as you strive for something that is important to you in the future and support your personal growth and development. Above all, having purpose strengthens your sense of self and is good for your health and well-being.

Your personal mission statement

Think about your purpose: what is your personal mission statement? When you figure out your personal mission statement, you will find it easier to make career and lifestyle choices. It can cover anything: family, health, relationships, etc.

Here are a few steps for defining your personal mission statement.

Be selective – choose a few topics to concentrate on and be specific. For example, determine where you want to work, or what hours you are prepared to work.

Write down your values along with your beliefs and intentions. We look in more detail at values in the next section.

Use positive language – "I will" and "I am" are better than "I want".

Your personal mission statement helps you understand what you care about and what you want for the future. Here are a few examples of personal mission statements to get you started.

"I take time every day for reflection, to realise what I've learnt, what I should learn, to say thank you, to give myself a pat on the back while looking at what I need to improve upon."

"I place great importance on being motivated and fulfilled by my job. If I am not happy at work and it is impacting my well-being, I will do something about it."

"I value the opportunity to learn and grow, and when I receive feedback or criticism I will treat it as a positive learning experience."

And here are a few from famous people for inspiration:

"To be a teacher. And to be known for inspiring my students to be more than they thought they could be."
Oprah Winfrey

"To have fun in my journey through life and learn from mistakes."
Sir Richard Branson, Entrepreneur

"I want to make it so that every person in the world can afford to start their own business."
John Rampton, Entrepreneur

Find it! Passion creates purpose

I enjoyed a successful career within the hotel industry. Whenever I took on a new role I felt energised and motivated with a strong sense of purpose in terms of what I wanted to achieve and how I would go about achieving it. I was clearly focused on the task in hand and totally engaged in fulfilling my purpose.

However, during my last year as CEO, I began to feel a little lost in terms of what I wanted, less energised and motivated about what the future would look like if I stayed in my current role. I challenged my sense of purpose and realised that it had changed. I realised that I wanted to do something about it to positively influence the future for both myself and the company

I decided to step down from the company, and ever since I have found a new purpose in life. I have been energised by my new challenges, taking a great sense of pride and satisfaction from following my passion and graduating as a leadership coach to help others fulfil their own potential. I have regained my sense of purpose, and as a result my life is easier, less complicated, less stressful and more meaningful.

Having a strong sense of purpose can have a powerful positive effect on you. Continually challenge yours.

Personal values

Values are a set of principles or ideas that are important to you in how you go about living your life. They act as a support, help you make decisions and guide and influence you. Your personal values give you structure and purpose by helping you to determine what is meaningful to you, your priorities. They tell others who you are and what you believe in and can act as a measure as to whether you are acting or living your life in the way you would like.

Your values can impact every aspect of your life, including:

- Where you want your life to go and how you want to live it
- The decisions you make
- Your personal behaviours and the approach you take
- How you interact with others, in and outside the work place.

When you know and embrace your own personal values you can use them as a measure to make decisions about how to fulfil your potential in areas that matter to you most. Your personal values will help you answer important career questions such as: is this the right job for me? Shall I accept this promotion? What decision should I take regarding leaving the company? Shall I follow a tradition route or travel down a new path?

Own it! Your purpose might change; your values are your cornerstone

Early on in my career, my purpose was to work hard to earn sufficient money to create a stable and secure environment for my family. Over time my career became an increasingly important part of my life and I assumed more responsibility for others – my team, my business, the organisation I was working for. My purpose had changed and evolved to become more inclusive.

I have always believed in a strong set of personal values which have remained consistent and have helped me to lead a team and run a business in a consistent, genuine and authentic way. My personal values are just as important in a business context as they are in my personal life.

However, what I place value on has changed over time. One of my reasons for stepping down from my CEO role was to realign and focus on what was important to me at that time– to spend more time with my family, to create a better work/life balance for myself and to broaden my knowledge and skills in an area that excites and motivates me. The personal values that were instrumental in my success during my career in hospitality are now the essential cornerstones of my coaching business.

Your purpose can change over time but your personal values remain part of you.

How do you know what your values are?

There are many exercises and tools to help you define your values. Although tools are useful, I believe that as you grow, both personally and professionally, your values will become clearer through your experiences.

In business, much time is spent on agreeing the values of the company, but I can't recall a time that I sat down with the purpose of agreeing my own personal values. Over time I have recognised them, acknowledged them and consciously embraced them.

There is no start or finish, no correct or ideal time, no definitive list. Here are four steps that will get you started:

1 Identify the times you were happiest, when you were most proud and when you were most fulfilled and satisfied, both from your career and your personal life
2 Determine your top values, based on your experiences of happiness, pride and fulfilment. Ask yourself the reasons why each experience is important and memorable
3 Prioritise the values that mean the most to you. Compare each value against the others to create a list in order of importance to you
4 Reaffirm your values by ensuring your choices and decisions align with your life and your vision for yourself.

Selected personal values list

Look at the (incomplete) list of personal values, add any that you think are missing and then select between five and ten that feel right for you and are important and integral to you.

Authenticity	Growth	Knowledge
Achievement	Happiness	Leadership
Adventure	Integrity	Learning
Authority	Love	Responsibility
Autonomy	Loyalty	Security
Balance	Meaningful Work	Self-Respect
Boldness	Openness	Service
Compassion	Optimism	Stability
Challenge	Peace	Success
Citizenship	Pleasure	Support
Community	Poise	Trustworthiness
Competency	Popularity	Wealth
Contribution	Recognition	Wisdom
Creativity	Religion	Humour
Curiosity	Reputation	
Determination	Respect	
Fairness	Honesty	
Faith	Influence	
Fame	Inner Harmony	
Friendships	Justice	
Fun	Kindness	

Be aware of the importance of your personal values and start to recognise them consciously so that you can embrace them and make decisions based around them.

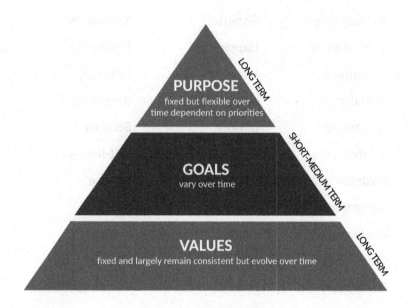

Corporate vision and values

Corporate purpose is essential to the success of a business, providing clear direction and intent in terms of what is important to the business going forward. Employees can be genuinely inspired if their business has a compelling vision and a clear, worthwhile mission. Visions and mission statements set out your purpose to customers, suppliers and the media, and can be highly motivating when they are expressed clearly and with intent and communicated effectively to everyone in the business.

"Good business leaders create a vision, articulate the vision, passionately own the vision, and relentlessly drive it to completion."

Jack Welch, Chairman of General Electric

What a company stands for and where a company is heading can be articulated and badged in many ways. The most common approach focuses on two key messages:

Mission statement defines the business's purpose and primary objectives. These statements are set in the present tense, and they explain why the organisation exists as a business both to staff and to people outside it. Mission statements tend to be short, clear and powerful.

Vision statement also defines a business's purpose, but focuses on its goals and aspirations. These statements are designed to be uplifting and inspiring. They're also timeless: even if the business changes its strategy, the vision will often stay the same.

Work it! Visions and values create success

Not every company I have worked for has recognised the importance of having a robust vision and a set of core values to support it, but the more successful companies have. When I was a Regional Director managing a team of sixteen General Managers, we created our own team values and vision. The process proved to be motivational, enlightening and productive and created a real sense of ownership and commitment to what we, as a team, were going to achieve and how we were going to do it.

Following healthy discussion and debate, we would agree on three key areas of focus supported by three key actions under each area, which gave the region clarity of direction and purpose. We also agreed our regional values and how we would work together as a team to achieve these. The key focus areas were measurable, we reviewed progress, and our values were reinforced at our monthly regional meeting, providing clarity to the questions: "What do we want to achieve?" and "How will we achieve it?"

Create your own team, department or company values. Having team ownership and commitment to deliver the agreed vision and values can lead to greater achievements and long-term success.

Corporate values or guiding principles underpin the vision and mission statements and explain how the business and its people go about fulfilling the company's purpose. They shape the culture and reflect what the company values. They are the essence of the company's identity – its guiding principles and beliefs. Establishing a strong set of core values can bring both internal and external advantages to a company:

- They educate and inform clients and potential clients about the company and what it stands for
- They can create competitor advantage
- They can be used as an essential recruiting and retention tool
- They support the decision making process, ensuring decisions are in alignment with values.
- They create a sense of pride and ownership within the business – a sense of belonging.

Make your vision and values mean something

Throughout my career, I have been part of many vision and values exercises and initiatives. They have all been different, some inspiring and impactful to the employees and the business, and others just a paper exercise, paying lip service with no real meaning or commitment.

Whether you are the CEO or head up a small team within the business, and whether you are talking about your company vision, mission statement, company purpose, guiding principles or core values, it is essential that you make the vision and values have real meaning and come alive. I recommend that you cut through all the words of intent and explanations and filter the message down to two key points for consideration:

What are we trying to achieve?

How do we go about achieving it?

Make the vision and values mean something to you and your team. Ensure that there is clarity, simplicity and that they are relevant. I have seen too many top level initiatives that haven't clearly translated through the business to the employees in terms of "What does this mean to me?" or "What do I need to do differently?" As a result nothing changes and the vision and values become almost irrelevant and meaningless.

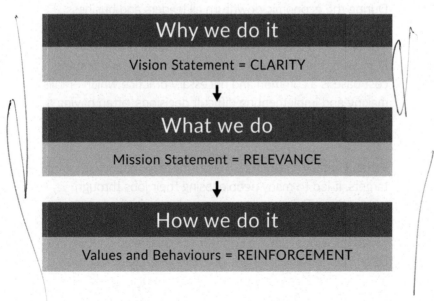

The Seven Habits of Highly Effective People by Stephen Covey has a chapter called "Begin with the End in Mind" which asserts that you must envision what you want in the future so you can work and plan towards it. The end is your purpose, your vision, what you are trying to achieve, and then you work back from that in terms of how you're going to do it.

A robust and meaningful vision and values initiative takes a significant amount of time, resource, commitment and perseverance to embed fully into a business and become a way of life. Values can be compromised for short-term gain, and the challenge for many leaders and companies is to balance short-term decisions and financial considerations with long-term vision and purpose. Once values are compromised, especially by leaders within the business, the negative impact can overshadow all the positives and good intent.

Work it! Values help to manage difficult decisions

During the economic downturn all leaders and business owners were facing the same challenge: how to make their business as resilient as possible for it to survive and prosper. Reviewing the resources of the business and reducing the cost base is a common and necessary practice which entails making and implementing difficult decisions, often having a personal and damaging impact on people, their family and their lives.

When I had to restructure the business to meet cost saving targets, it led to many people losing their jobs through redundancy. These were team members who had worked hard and were committed, but as leaders we have to take tough decisions that are right for the business – not just for us or the individual. My key purpose when handling the restructure was to treat everyone with empathy, compassion and professionalism in line with my values and the values of the company. The message may have been hard to give, but the way that it was delivered and the support I could offer was important to me, and the values of the company to treat everyone as individuals and with respect played an important role in the successful handling of the redundancy programme.

When faced with difficult challenges and problems, allow your values to support and guide you in making the right decisions.

Successful companies and leaders ensure that everyone understands the part they have to play in working towards fulfilling the vision. They lead from the front, are totally committed and take every opportunity to make the vision and values an integral part of the way the business operates.

How to make it stick – reinforcement

Once the company purpose, supported by a vision and a set of core values, has been agreed and communicated, the challenge is to get it embedded and embraced through all levels within the business – to make it stick and become part of the culture.

Take every opportunity to reaffirm and reinforce the vision and values:

- Walk the talk – lead by example and personally deliver them on a consistent basis
- Refer to them in regular communication initiatives and company or departmental newsletters, giving examples of

how the vision and values have been brought to life through employee and customer stories

- Structure daily and weekly meeting agendas around them
- Recognise and reward good practice and champions
- Make them an integral part of the recruitment and induction process
- Include them in your individual and team objectives and focus areas
- Make them visible through internal posters, prompt cards, mugs, mouse mats and screen savers
- Base performance reviews and appraisals around them with clear expectations of what "great" looks like.

Work it! Get everyone on board

The "Commitment to Quality" initiative that I championed within Macdonald Hotels proved to be the foundation of successfully changing the culture and focus of the business. The brief from the Board was clear: while the business was renowned for its strong track record of financial success and profitability, the focus and culture of the company required a step change to support quality of service and employee engagement in equal measure.

Following a structured and inclusive approach which encouraged input from all levels within the business, from the Board to focus groups within hotels, we introduced a clear vision and set of values to the business: "Commitment to Quality – People. Service. Results". For the next six years this new approach was communicated, reinforced and practised. It was positively embraced and gave balance, perspective and a clear sense of direction to what the business stood for and what it wanted to achieve.

Its success was also due to it being clear, simple, relevant, and everyone able to articulate the part they could play to allow the business to fulfil its potential. Once the culture evolved and developed internally, our reputation improved externally. Profitability continued to grow on an annual basis despite the challenging economic times, and the company enjoyed its highest levels of people engagement.

Two years after the "Commitment to Quality" initiative was launched, Macdonald Hotels was recognised as AA Hotel Group of the Year for delivering high levels of customer service and quality of product.

Company culture and reputation can be changed if the vision and values of a company are meaningful and relevant to everyone and lived by everyone.

Recruit to values

What happens when your personal values are different from the business values? What happens if you recruit people who don't share your business's values?

If your **personal values** don't fit with the business and the culture that you find yourself in then you may feel uncomfortable and have more difficulty reaching your potential. Your personal values help you to make decisions that are right for you and influence the approach that you take. When you're considering if a company is right for you, if the culture is a good fit, or if you will be managed and treated in a way that will maximise your potential, consider mapping your own values against the business's values to see if they are consistent with one another.

As a manager or leader, aim to **recruit to values** and you will avoid possible problems with value misalignment. When you're interviewing always consider the values and culture of the business to give you a better chance of making an informed recruitment decision. By recruiting to values you will know almost intuitively what decisions the successful candidate will make and how they will go about working in the business. The values of a business create its culture, and if an employee's values are not aligned with that culture, they will struggle to be comfortable and will lack the capacity and motivation to fulfil their potential.

Find it! The right cultural fit

I have worked with many talented individuals who found themselves within a culture that was not right for them. When the values of a company and the way individuals are managed and treated aren't conducive to them performing at their best, they find themselves becoming demotivated and lacking energy to drive themselves and the business. They can begin to lose confidence in their own ability to be successful.

By finding an environment that is consistent with their values and approach, people can quickly change from being a poor performer to a leading performer, creating a strong future for themselves.

Take time to find the right fit for you and others. Individual and organisational potential can be more effectively realised when values and the culture are aligned.

Summary

Agreeing a purpose with supporting values provides a cornerstone for planned and effective growth and progress. Your values will form part of you and your business and will provide direction to you going forward, helping you decide what you want and why you want it.

"If the ladder is not leaning against the right wall, every step we take just gets us to the wrong place faster."

Stephen Covey, Author

CHAPTER 5

What do you want and why?

"If you don't design your own life plan, chances are
you'll fall into someone else's plan. And guess what
they have planned for you? Not much."

Jim Rohn, Entrepreneur

In a business context, it's quite common to explain your purpose, to have a vision and know where you're going. From a personal point of view, it's more of a challenging task to articulate your purpose. Not everyone will know what they want out of life and how they want their career to progress. Many people may still be asking themselves that question as they plod on in their existing job or career.

What's important to you?

Discovering what you really want to do with your life and your career requires a great deal of thought and energy and a challenging and open mind. If you take an approach from a business point of view and apply it to a personal point of view, a strong vision and knowing what you want can help you actually get it.

Find it! What's your goal?

I had never thought about working in a hotel, but I had always envisaged myself working with others and being part of a team. Having been an overseas travel representative for three years after leaving college, I wanted to continue within that sector, but I had no idea what that looked like and what it could lead to.

Once I started working in a hotel, I knew what I wanted. I had a clear goal. I had found my purpose. My goal was to become a Hotel General Manager by the time I was thirty years old. As a trainee working in my first hotel, I was excited and motivated about the idea of having the responsibility for a business and leading a team of people to success. I was encouraged because I could see the steps required to climb up the ladder. I had a plan and was determined to work hard to achieve my goal.

I was appointed to my first General Manager position at the age of twenty-eight, two years ahead of my plan. It was then time to set the next goal for myself and to start planning to achieve it.

Always try to set yourself a goal of where you want to be. Achieving your initial goal can provide a foundation for future and greater success.

Have a plan, but be flexible

Some of us will go with the flow, go wherever our career takes us. Others will want to be more in control. They'll know what they want, why they want it, and then go out with a focused approach to making it happen.

If you are in the first group, perhaps struggling to know where you want your career to go or how to influence a change in career, try this simple exercise:

Think about where you want to be in five years' time. This helps you to focus on what is important to you: where do you see yourself? What do you see yourself doing? To make that become reality, work backwards to determine what actions you need to take and what skills you will require to fulfil your vision.

The idea of seeing into the future and picturing where you'll be in five years' time isn't straightforward. The chances of visualising it correctly are very slim, but this exercise does help you to focus the mind and consolidate your thinking. It might be easier to reverse the process and ask yourself what you **don't** want to be doing or where you **don't** want to be in five years' time.

"Where do you want to be in five years' time?" is a common interview question as it gives an indication of how ambitious and forward-thinking an individual is.

Create your own luck

I believe that you can create and influence your own luck by working hard, delivering results and treating people in a professional manner, but I also believe that some people get lucky breaks – just as I did. It's important, however, to make the most of those lucky breaks.

Own it! Make the most of opportunities

There's a lot to be said for being in the right place at the right time. I have been very fortunate in my career; many colleagues and friends have struggled to fulfil their potential even though they are capable of more because they haven't had that lucky break. Keep an open mind if new job approaches are made to you or opportunities are offered. Don't rest on your laurels just because you have been given an opportunity. Continually push yourself and find ways to grow and develop. Don't be afraid to ask for help and support when required.

One of the greatest pleasures I get in business is to see individuals and teams embrace and make the most of the opportunities that they have been given and to use them as a platform to progress their careers.

Make the most of the opportunities that you are presented with. Work hard and continually prove yourself to create your own luck so other opportunities come your way.

Be – Do – Have

Most people tend to follow the Do – Have – Be approach, believing "If I do what I do, I'll get what I want to have and then I can be the person I've always wanted to be." However, the challenge that arises is that the person you have always been is not going to think, act or react in a way that is going to get you to your goal.

What if we looked at the process differently? **Be – Do – Have**. It is a subtle change but one that can have significant impact. **Be** the person you would be if you'd already achieved your goal, then you

will **do** the things that a successful person would do, which will allow you more readily to **have** exactly what you want.

The Be – Do – Have approach helps to simplify how you go about being what you want to be. It places more emphasis on **being who** you want to be by behaving and acting as if your goal has already been achieved.

If your goal is to become more confident so as to create more opportunities for yourself going forward, then how would you be acting if you'd achieved that? How would you be presenting yourself to others? What would you be telling yourself? Act in a confident and self-assured way to fulfil your goal. Start "being" now!

Work it! Get what you want through the success of others

I've worked with some ambitious General Managers who were very focused on developing their career and rising through the ranks within the company. Higher status and being seen as successful proved to be, rightly or wrongly, their overriding goal and objective.

I gave them some advice: "Focus all your energies on your business being successful rather than on you being successful. Instead of seizing every opportunity to increase your own profile and share your future aspirations and ambitions, let the performance of the business and your team make the difference. In turn, this will reflect on you, providing you with the platform to achieve what you want to achieve personally."

This is advice that I learnt from my own approach as I grew within the business, and on reflection it served me well. If you channel your energies into your team and the business being successful, this can then support you and others and influence where you want to be in the future.

Focus your energies on the team and your business being successful rather than focusing solely on your own agenda and profile. What you want to achieve and what you want to be will come through the success of others and your business.

Take control

We can all let events and our "to do" lists take over. Soon weeks, months and years blur into one another and become a continuous loop. However, it's never too late to take charge – to manage yourself and influence your future. Be proactive and take control.

We will have differing views on how much control we have over our destiny. Some believe that they have little or no control over the future which results in them swimming with the tide and going where they are taken. Others will believe that they are totally in control of shaping their future.

Locus of control – internal versus external control

The locus of control is a simple business model, devised by Julian Rotter, to assess where you are on the locus of control range. It describes the degree to which people perceive that outcomes result either from their own behaviour or from forces external to themselves. This produces a continuum with external control at one end and internal control at the other.

INTERNAL
You make things happen.
You control your destiny.

EXTERNAL
Things happen to you.
They control your destiny.

The results of Rotter's research suggest that the most successful individuals possess a high level of internal locus of control. They believe their actions make things happen and they are responsible for their own success. Individuals with a high internal locus of control tend to recognise the importance of a positive mindset, work hard to develop their knowledge and skills, and adopt a more participative management style.

On the other end of the scale, people with a high external locus of control believe that external forces determine their outcome. They tend to wait for the lucky breaks.

Being in control – finding clarity and direction in respect of what you want both personally and professionally in your career – can be a challenge. Knowing what you want and what's best for you and motivates you is not always easy to determine. What you want can also change over time. Gone are the days when a job was for life and you stayed within the same career. Career development is not just about gaining the skills and experience to advance within a business, but more importantly it's about being flexible and continually evaluating and developing your skills to remain employable, motivated and fulfilled.

Our motivations and ambitions vary greatly. We are all different, so the challenge is to understand fully what motivates **you** – why you are motivated and what you want from work.

Career control

Edgar Schein is a leading career psychologist who created "Career Anchors" to help people assess an individual's preference and motivations. Schein has identified eight career factors. He believes that everyone has a "dominant career anchor", and that by understanding and identifying your own dominant career anchor, you will be better placed to determine the career, role and environment that will give you the best fit and most satisfaction.

The eight career anchors are:

Technical/functional – motivated by being really good at something, specialising, highly skilled professional or expert in a particular field.

General managerial – not specialist, generalists, good at delegating, problem solving and directing others.

Independence and autonomy – like to make their own rules, set their own standards, work independently.

Security and stability – risk avoiders who prefer calm, stable environments, generally competent.

Entrepreneurial creativity – inventive, creative, energetic people who enjoy working with others to achieve a dream.

Service or dedication to a cause – motivated by work that appeals to their core values, even if it isn't taking advantage of their skills.

Pure challenge – competitive problem solvers, always looking for the next big challenge.

Lifestyle – work to live, have a good balance with work and life.

Schein's career anchors may prove a useful tool to explore what's important to you in your career. You can go online to take the test at: www.career anchor online.com

Summary

Knowing what you want and why you want it requires a concentrated and planned thought process. However, many careers are shaped by people taking advantage of opportunities as they arise. It can be liberating and exciting to have an open mind about the future, although many of us will be anxious about not being in control and will have a strong need to plan to make it happen.

"Your present circumstances don't determine
where you can go; they merely determine
where you start from."

Nido Qubein, Author

CHAPTER 6

Get specific and make it happen

"Some people want it to happen, some wish it would
happen, others make it happen."
Michael Jordan

In the previous chapters, we've talked about the importance of having a vision or a strong purpose to support you in moving forward and reaching the potential that you have inside you. In order for the vision to be successful and come to life, a clear plan with a strategy for making that plan happen will make a significant difference.

Visualise – Plan – Implement – Review

Visualise where you are going and what you want to achieve and agree a clear goal and a target. Plan how you can go about achieving it through strategies and tactics and implement them energetically to make it happen. Review your progress against your goals and consider how close you are to your target. The model is circular – you continue around it, always with your goal balanced and in mind.

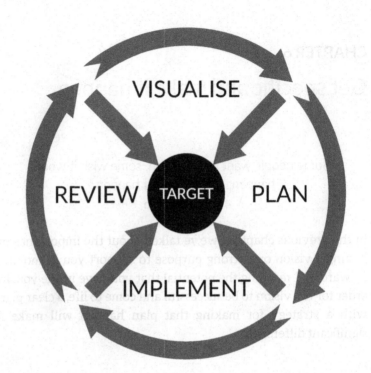

In most cases, if one of the four elements is missing then the task becomes harder and less clear. While you won't spend equal amounts of time in each element, a balanced approach to all elements is critical to success. The implementation stage is perhaps the most challenging and usually takes the most execution time, but it's also the most important.

I've witnessed many action plans, strategy documents, profit improvement plans, personal development plans, but would question how much has been successfully implemented as a result of them. We can spend a lot of our time visualising and producing impressive plans, but if little time is spent on implementation, then the whole thing falls apart. Why spend time and energy planning and not follow through to make it happen? Shift the balance towards taking action and making it happen or all the planning time is wasted energy.

In a business context, sometimes the planning stage can be overlooked. You may be told to "make it happen" or to get on with reaching a target or take some form of action without any planned approach or supporting guidelines. Again, the process becomes unbalanced and can lead to confusion, inconsistency and minimal impact or progress. It can also lead to resentment and disengagement as a lack of supporting guidelines in the implementation stage can imply that the **How** has not been thought through effectively and that the end target may be unrealistic and unachievable.

Why targets and goals are important

Set out your expectations on what needs to be achieved clearly and then commit to daily, weekly or monthly targets – whatever is most relevant and meaningful to the review process.

The targeting approach can apply to all levels within the business – at departmental level or for anyone who has responsibility to deliver results from a team of people. However, ineffective targeting and not following through will have a detrimental impact, creating disengagement and resulting in a lack of credibility.

Own it! Set targets you want to meet and exceed

I learnt so much from my team and I recognised a specific strength in each of them that I respected, admired and tried to emulate.

I worked alongside a Leisure and Spa Director who was a master of targeting and displayed a relentless drive and energy to deliver results. Every month, without fail, she set targets per club and spa for various areas of the business, tracking the progress. She communicated weekly and monthly league tables together with a supportive commentary on who was doing well, sharing best practice and putting pressure on the poorer performers to improve. She also held conference calls to reinforce the message and to create a culture of support and encouragement within the team.

This approach became a culture, a way of doing business, and resulted in the clubs and spas invariably exceeding budgets and targets. The targets provided a focus, a measure of success, and maximised the potential within the business.

Effective, consistent targeting can drive exceptional performance but only if you own, commit, and drive the process. You are then in a position to let your results "do the talking".

There's a skill in making targets effective and meaningful so they add value to your business. Here are some of my learnings and best practices:

- Make the targets challenging yet achievable
- Break down your overall target into manageable, clear, measurable amounts and then add a little to create an over-target to ensure delivery
- Be clear about who is responsible for delivering – hold them accountable
- Ensure you track and communicate progress on a regular basis
- Learn from the best performers and share best practice continually to drive and improve performance levels
- Be consistent with the process. Don't set a target with no follow-up or review as the next targeting exercise will have no credibility
- Recognise and reward the relevant person/team once targets are exceeded
- Keep the process alive through messages, calls and keeping the team focused and motivated
- Set "super targets" during the month to push performance more if targets are either easily exceeded or proving to be unrealistic and demotivating.

Work it! Short term and simple

Effective targeting linked to incentives and rewards provides motivation and focus; it can add significant value to the business, especially when the targets are sales related.

I have found that a clear, measurable and short term approach to setting targets yields the best results. Teams are usually more enthused and motivated by daily and weekly targets that can be easily understood and clearly measured, and where their efforts in reaching the target can be quickly recognised and rewarded.

Short term targets also help to keep the interest and motivation of the team and allow for the key target areas to flex depending on the current needs of the business.

Keep targets short term, clear and measurable to yield the best results

Get noticed

Although I stayed within one industry and followed a traditional career path, this is not as common in today's world with the impact of technology, globalisation and new ways of doing business. Career paths need to be created, managed and influenced through one or multiple organisations. Your career plan, achievements and future potential need to be understood, recognised and nurtured by you and others. Career advancement is not a given – you need to **take control and influence people**.

Spend time on succeeding and excelling in your current position, but also spend time on influencing, both internally and externally, and getting noticed to help build your future. If people don't know what you are capable of and what you have already achieved, then you may miss the opportunity to be considered for new opportunities, be part of a project or get recognised for your hard work. Don't always keep your head down and quietly get on with it – make yourself as visible as possible for all the right reasons.

Own it! Are you ready? Do you have enough experience?

I have been asked many times for my advice on whether someone should apply for a new role within an organisation. My usual response is: "What have you got to lose?"

A Deputy Manager was put forward for me to interview for a General Manager's position. I didn't know much about him, and from his CV I felt he didn't have the level of experience and the successful track record that this position required. Although he knew his chance of success was limited, he grasped the opportunity to demonstrate that he was ambitious, that he wanted to get noticed, and during the interview he was able to explain many of his achievements that weren't visible on his CV. He was now on my radar and had got himself noticed.

I was impressed with him, but I didn't feel he was the right fit for the position on offer, and deep down I don't think he did either. He was, however, the right fit for another position that was due to be circulated later that month

Push yourself forward and make a good impression. Get in front of people who can support you to get what you are working towards.

How to get noticed

Build relationships – help people out, look for opportunities to help others advance, then when you need assistance you will have a group of people around you who take an interest in helping you.

Put yourself forward – don't hide in the shadows. Contribute, make yourself heard and take credit for your achievements.

Network internally and externally – create allies within the whole organisation and in your field. Put yourself in others' minds as you never know what opportunities may arise.

Be and have a mentor – they can assist you with getting noticed as they have probably had the same issues to deal with. Being a mentor creates allies and builds your reputation and credibility.

Get close to your boss – work out how you can help them achieve their goals. Ensure they know what you've achieved and where you want your career to go.

Be hungry for development – always be improving and learning.

Challenge positively – it's important to acknowledge others' points of view, and to put forward your own ideas in an enthusiastic and collaborative way. Make your voice heard.

Embrace the culture – join in with the teamwork activities and the out-of-hours chances to network and socialise.

Talk yourself up – don't be too modest. Sell yourself when you need to, but always consider the importance of a balanced approach and talk up others too.

Be proactive – create your own opportunities. Look for gaps, be the solution to potential problems.

Work it! Be visible

When I was Regional Director of Forte Heritage Hotels with responsibility for over 1,000 people, I made it my business to meet and get to know as many members of the team as I could. I have always placed importance on building and developing relationships at all levels.

However, a certain chef made it his business to get to know me.

From the kitchen, he made a point of coming front of house, taking opportunities to become visible whenever I was visiting the hotel. He would update me on the progress in his kitchen, talk up the successes and invite me to taste new dishes. He effectively developed a relationship with me, so I sought him out, asking his opinion and getting him involved in regional projects. He soon became the chef I would turn to within the region and was later promoted to Regional Catering Manager.

A few years later, he became Catering Director for the whole group and his career has gone from strength to strength. On reflection, I realise he successfully put himself forward without pushing himself forward. He made himself visible to me and positively influenced his future by getting himself noticed and building a relationship. He also allowed his results, his passion and his commitment to do the talking, which I very much admired.

Make yourself visible with the intention to influence your future potential positively.

When you get noticed and become more visible, you create an opportunity to influence. Find ways to influence upwards to demonstrate that you are ready for a promotion or to become a manager with increased responsibility. Focus on the areas that help you get noticed and build on them.

While we've looked at ways of getting yourself noticed for all the right reasons, there are plenty of pitfalls and signs that will tell your boss that you are not right for promotion. Can you recognise any of the following within yourself or your team?

- Doing the minimum every day, just enough to get by
- Being insular and not a team player
- Being negative about the business and moaning to others
- Relying on your current base of knowledge rather than putting yourself forward for additional development
- Taking all the credit for any successes
- Expecting a promotion rather than influencing one.

If any of the above resonate with you then you will need to review your approach and do something differently to change others' perception of you. If your team members fall into any of the above then challenge them to become more self-aware and help them to help themselves.

The Will in the GROW model

The GROW model used in coaching is a process designed to discover what you want to achieve and how you are going to achieve it. We look in more depth at the GROW model in "Chapter 9: Coach to Success and Listen".

The last stage of the model is the Will – the stage of commitment and implementation of the agreed actions, or making it happen. Typical questions that encourage and gain commitment include:

- What are you going to do?
- When are you going to do it?
- Will this course of action achieve your goal?
- Which of these actions are most important?
- What support is required?
- What are the potential barriers and how are they overcome?
- When are you going to review the progress towards your goal?

Motivation

Motivation is the inner power that pushes you towards taking action and gets you to your goals. It is powered by desire and ambition, so if they are absent, motivation is absent too. Even though you might want to get things done and achieve your targets, if your desire isn't strong enough you will lack the willingness to take action. Action is what makes it happen.

On the other hand, when you are motivated you have internal drive, energy, enthusiasm and persistence to follow through and achieve your goals and targets. You take action. Your motivation gets stronger when you have a vision and a plan.

Motivation is one of the most important behaviours to success. Lack of motivation leads to mediocre or, worse, no results. You will find out in the Review stage of the model whether your motivation is strong enough to fulfil your goals and targets and whether you are motivated enough to try a different course of action or start again

Motivate yourself to take action and make it happen

Everyone can find excuses for not doing something. We may procrastinate because we are too busy or we just don't have the necessary inner drive to get something started and then completed.

Some tips that I have found useful to get myself motivated:

Tell others what you intend to do – they can then support and motivate you on your journey. They can also put some pressure on you as you have set an expectation in their minds.

Get tough with yourself – be accountable to yourself and set a high level of self-expectation. Visualise and feel your disappointment and frustration if your action is limited or half-hearted.

Create a plan with celebration milestones – set realistic and achievable goals with short time frames and celebrate their completion.

Simplify and prioritise your "to do" list – try not to make an exhaustive list that might overwhelm or demotivate you. Prioritise a couple of actions that will help you to take a step towards your plan and feel good when you have completed them. Tackle a particular action that has been on the list for a long time.

Remove the barriers to action – identify and challenge your thinking to discard any potential barriers you may have created. Focus on the How rather than the If.

Energise yourself to action – change your mindset to become energised by action and progress rather than allowing the thought and process to drain your energy levels.

Create the right environment – clear your desk to help clear your mind.

Own it! Get motivated

I have always had great ideas which energise me, but finding the motivation to get things done through to the completion stage has always been a challenge for me as usually I have already moved onto the next idea. I recognise that I am not the best "completer finisher".

However, I was determined to make this book happen and I have approached the task in a planned and structured way. I gained support from a book coach who gave me direction, and together we set targets and milestones to work towards. The book was broken down into manageable chunks to write. My book cover was designed and created at the outset, which gave me inspiration as I wrote the content.

I also told a handful of trusted and respected colleagues and friends of my intention, and their support, encouragement and interest during the process has made me more determined to make it happen. By involving them, I created an expectation that I would deliver the book within the timescale I had set.

Find ways that motivate you and keep you focused and you will be capable of more than you realise.

Summary

Delivering results and pushing forward is dependent on being clear about what you need to achieve and then taking action to make it happen. It sounds simplistic, but taking the relevant action to effect a desirable outcome can be challenging and involved.

To keep focused and motivated on the target, you have to set and adopt a results-orientated approach to improve performance.

"The path to success is to take
massive determined action."
Tony Robbins, Author

CHAPTER 7

Be the best you can

> "The supreme quality for leadership is unquestionably integrity. Without it no real success is possible..."
>
> **Dwight D Eisenhower**

Whenever I am asked what key message I can pass down to aspiring leaders or managers I always come back to this: "Be the best you can and lead by example. Lead from the front, treat others in a respectful manner and conduct yourself with the utmost professionalism and integrity."

Whether you are a graduate trainee, a supervisor of a department or the General Manger, your reputation and the respect you can gain evolves through each career step you take. **Behaviour breeds behaviour and influences your reputation.** Aim to be a role model for the business and for the next generation of leaders.

Lead by example

Many leaders fail to recognise or perhaps underestimate the impact that they **personally** have on their teams or the business. I have seen the significant impact that a senior executive or chairman can have by just talking to and taking a personal interest in their employees or fellow team members. The value an employee receives from that recognition can be immense. It can help to shape and influence their thoughts and opinions about the business that they are working for.

As a result they start working for you as the leader, not just for the company, and feel a sense of ownership, belonging and loyalty.

In many industries it's typical for managers and leaders to be seen visiting the factory or shop floor. These are opportunities for leaders to get a closer feel for the business and experience the service for themselves rather than seeing everything on a spreadsheet or a customer service report. These visits can also be an opportunity to lead by example and communicate with team members at all levels, engaging with them to understand more about them as individuals and to show appreciation for their hard work, efforts and achievements.

The reverse approach, however, can have a significant and damaging impact. An executive, representing the company, who is cold, distant and uncommunicative and displays a total disregard for people can have far reaching implications for the business. Employees start to feel less valued and unimportant, and as a result I have seen a fear culture evolve, leaving team members disengaged and demotivated.

Leaders at all levels need to display elements of humanity and humility with their teams and their colleagues, just as we'd expect them to do with their customers.

> "Leaders with integrity act with authenticity and honesty by speaking the truth, presenting themselves in a genuine way with sincerity, showing no pretense and taking responsibility for their own feelings and actions."
> *Character Strengths and Virtues*, Peterson and Seligman

It can be easy at times to become complacent and take advantage of the position that we have been given as a leader, especially in light of the pressure and demands that come with increased responsibility and leading teams or a business. However, inspirational leaders effectively manage to avoid this complacency. If you are a leader, put yourself in the shoes of others and try to see what they see.

Own it! Lead by example

An ex-colleague who worked with me for over twenty-five years is a great example of a leader who epitomised **leading by example**. She has strong personal values, high levels of integrity and is consistent in her approach. She "walked the talk". Her employees knew what she stood for and where they stood with her. She developed a strong following of like-minded people who wanted to be on her team, remained loyal and committed to her, and wanted to be part of her success. It was no coincidence that her region consistently out-performed in terms of profitability, employee engagement and customer quality.

Leaders who lead by example create and influence a culture of success and high performance. Your reputation is merely who others think you are, but your character is who you really are.

To lead by example, you must be very clear on your personal and company values. We talked in Chapter 4: The Importance of Purpose, about values and having a strong sense of purpose for yourself and the business, and it is when leading others that you will need to pull on these attributes. Great leaders will consistently demonstrate their values in how they conduct themselves on a day to day basis, personally and professionally. They will refer to those values and use them to make decisions in the business, supported by solid reasoning, rather than taking decisions which could be personal, impulsive, inconsistent and irresponsible.

Not all decisions will be the right ones. Everyone can make poor decisions which at the time seem right. I have made many decisions that in hindsight proved to be wrong, and I'm sure I will continue to do so. The skill is to learn from your poor decisions and the mistakes that you make. If you want your team to be empowered, experiment and take risks then it is important to set a precedent and lead by example.

Create a culture that encourages forward thinking and trying new things, but freely admit when they don't work or haven't been successful. Demonstrate to your team that it's no bad thing to make mistakes. It's more important to react well to mistakes and implement what you learn from them.

The importance of integrity

Integrity is consistently rated as one of the most important character traits of a respected leader. It is often considered a given and the basis upon which all other leadership traits are built. **With integrity comes trust.** If you cannot rely on a leader to act with integrity and honesty, then how can you trust them and why work for them?

Integrity can be defined in various ways. Palanski and Yammarino ("Integrity in Organizations: Building the Foundations for Humanistic Management", 2007) in their review of over thirty articles that contain a definition of integrity, summarise:

"At the heart of integrity is being consistent, honest,
moral and trustworthy. Leaders with integrity are
unfailing with who they are and what they stand for."

For me integrity is about personal values, consistency of approach, admitting when you are wrong and doing what you believe is right. Consistently leading by example. **To be successful without integrity really isn't success at all.** Those with integrity keep their word, even when it's difficult or there is no personal gain. They make values-based decisions, concerned more about their character than their reputation. While no one is perfect, and we all make mistakes, those with integrity admit their mistakes and do what they can to right the wrong.

Develop resilience

All successful leaders must understand and embrace the importance of being resilient. From a business and personal perspective, we are invariably faced with unexpected barriers and challenges which require us to delve deep and discover our inner strengths to tackle them head on, not allowing problems to take us off course. The business world today comes with many challenges and setbacks. The best leaders know how to refocus, re-energise and remain determined to overcome them.

What is resilience?

Resilience is a quality that allows people to be knocked down by life and come back stronger than ever. Rather than letting failure and adversity overwhelm them and drain their resolve, successful, resilient leaders find a way to deal with challenges personally in a positive manner. **To create a resilient business, you need resilient teams led by resilient leaders.**

Being resilient means we have the strength to learn the lessons we need to learn, and the wisdom to move on to tackle further challenges from a position of strength and positivity. The most resilient teams and individuals aren't the ones that don't fail or haven't suffered any setbacks or adversity; they are the ones that fail, learn from the failures and thrive because of them.

What makes us resilient?

Psychologists have identified some of the factors that make people resilient. They have a positive attitude and mindset, are optimistic, have the ability to manage their emotions and see failure as a form of helpful feedback. They have a determined outlook and a clear sense of purpose supported by solid goals, and are driven. I particularly like the approach from Susan Kobasa, a leading psychologist who believes there are three key elements that are essential to resilience:

Challenge – adversity and difficulty are seen as challenges, not disasters. Resilient leaders accept that they will make mistakes and encounter problems, but they don't see this as a reflection of their worth; they see it as a challenge to grow and develop.

Commitment – with a purpose and a compelling reason to move forwards, resilient leaders make a commitment to their goals, their team and their business. And it's not just restricted to their business; they make strong commitments in their personal lives, to family and friends and their own well-being.

Personal control – resilient leaders understand the difference between the things in their control and those merely under their influence. They have the wisdom to know how to put their energies to good use to work on those things they have control over and not to worry about uncontrollable events.

What can you do to develop your resilience?

Resilience can be self-taught. Research indicates that resilience is built by attitudes and behaviours that can be adopted and implemented by anyone. How we view adversity and stress strongly affects how successful we are at dealing with it, and this highlights the importance of having a resilient and positive mindset and being open and capable of changing it to support the thinking process.

Individuals with a fixed mindset tend to find it more challenging to react in a positive manner when they encounter setbacks, failure or adversity. They see their outcomes as evidence of who they are and what they are capable of. People with "growth" mindsets tend to see outcomes as evidence of what they could improve upon in the future and what challenges they can overcome.

Being challenged or suffering from adversity can be part of what activates resilience as a skill set, and the ability to build resilience will serve you well in an increasingly stressful and demanding work culture where potential burnout is widespread. The environment we work in is not likely to change so it's becoming more important than ever to build resilience skills to manage your workload and any impact on your personal life effectively.

Some simple steps to start building your resilience:

Positive self-talk – try to see the good and not just the bad in all situations. Consistently practise positive thinking.

Take good care of yourself – get enough sleep and take regular exercise.

Learn from your mistakes and setbacks. Every mistake has the power to teach you something important, so don't dismiss mistakes, learn from them.

Maintain perspective. Try not to blow events out of proportion, nor to generalise. Be thankful for what you have.

Be in control. You have a choice as to how you respond to a situation. Your reaction is down to you.

Build your self-confidence. We look at this a little later in this chapter.

Set some goals that you can work towards. Monitor and acknowledge the progress you are making. Celebrate your success.

Above all, keep smiling and laughing.

Find it! Adversity can make you stronger

During my first General Manager appointment, I became a widower with a daughter less than a month old. I had to dig deep into my inner strength and reserves to cope both personally and professionally. I had a baby who needed me, a business to run and a team that depended on me. I had no choice but to adopt a strong, positive mindset to deal with the situation and I quickly found strength that I hadn't realised I possessed. I was determined to get through it as successfully as possible to prove to myself, my family, my team and my employer that I was resilient. Becoming a victim of my circumstances was not an option.

I have used that time in my life to draw on the strength that I know I now have. There have been many occasions since when I've found it a challenge to put setbacks, pressure and stress into perspective as invariably current reality kicks in, but I recognise that it is important to anchor what I have learnt and acknowledge how I have coped.

Adversity can make you stronger and more resilient if you allow it to.

What can businesses do to become more resilient?

Businesses also need to display resilience, especially during difficult and challenging times, for example during a downturn or implementing change. Effective leadership can build resilience in a business by coaching the team to take responsibility, take risks, learn from success and failure, and build self-confidence through praise and recognition. The more effective your team, the more resilient your business becomes. A strong, resilient business is well prepared and structured to deal with any form of adversity.

Work it! Develop resilience for the future

I was CEO of Macdonald Hotels during the financial crisis and economic downturn in 2008. The impact on the business was going to be significant with drastic cutbacks on corporate and personal spending. I was fortunate that my Chairman was intuitive and forward thinking as he had predicted the recession much earlier than others. That gave us time to be one step ahead and to plan accordingly.

We had to face up to the challenge and be prepared to make and take difficult decisions regarding the cost base in the business, which inevitably led to many people losing their jobs. Every area of the business was challenged in terms of how productivity and efficiency could be improved.

We remained determined and focused on what needed to be done, dealing with issues and challenges on a one by one basis, not allowing them to cloud our judgement or derail our strategy to achieve the overall goal that we had set. Our team rose to the challenge and supported the actions in a professional and robust manner as they had a clear understanding of the rationale and the goals of the exercise. The company came out stronger, leaner, more focused and more confident of the future.

Don't let challenges overwhelm you or your business. Be one step ahead and be prepared to take difficult decisions to make the business more resilient for the future.

Get out of your comfort zone

To be the best you can, many would argue that you need to leave your comfort zone to experience new challenges, learn and grow.

I would not describe myself as a risk taker, but I do like a challenge. I enjoyed continuous service with one company for nearly thirty years, albeit with five changes of ownership, remaining loyal to the company, the industry and my teams.

Throughout my career, I often wondered whether staying with the same company would be perceived as a strength or a weakness. Was I seen as loyal, resilient, good at building and maintaining relationships? Or did people think I was in my comfort zone, not ambitious, adverse to change, inflexible in my thought process?

If you stay with the same company or carry out the same role over a considerable time, you may begin to doubt your value in the marketplace and questions can develop in your mind as to whether you have the ability to thrive and succeed outside your current role or company. Society and business invariably demand we leave our comfort zone to challenge ourselves, see what we are capable of, take risks, but I believe that **there are benefits to staying in your comfort zone** as well. Everyone is different and there are strong cases for both arguments.

The positives of being in your comfort zone:

- It builds self-confidence and confidence in others
- You develop high levels of experience and knowledge of your environment
- It provides personal and professional stability
- You build strong and lasting relationships
- It could be the place and opportunity for you to make your greatest contribution
- You gain happiness and contentment by being true to yourself.

The benefits of challenging yourself outside of your comfort zone:

- You enjoy new experiences to build your resilience
- It can increase your confidence and may lead to higher levels of achievement both personally and professionally
- You gain more opportunities to learn new skills and continually grow and develop
- It can be motivational and exhilarating
- It allows you to be creative in your thinking and your approach
- You can build new relationships and grow your network
- It pushes you to perform at your best.

Although it may seem that I was in my comfort zone due to my continuous service, this was never the case. I can think of many examples where I was thrown in the deep end and had to either sink or swim. Although I am not a risk taker, I have faced and effectively dealt with many challenges.

All leaders will have experiences and examples of being out of their comfort zones – the challenge is to embrace them positively, deal with them confidently and professionally and learn from them.

Own it! It's never too late to make a change

Despite appearing potentially risk adverse, I have made a significant and intentional leap out of my comfort zone. I took the decision to step down from a role that provided a secure environment both professionally and financially to venture out on my own after nearly thirty years of continuous service. I never thought I would or could do it – but I have.

Despite my initial worries and concerns, I have surprised myself by how energised I feel and how motivated I have become. I see this new role as an opportunity to be true to myself and authentically define what I want out of life. My priorities have changed and I am now taking personal control of my future.

It's never too late to make a change, be it a small step or a giant leap. Getting out of your comfort zone and taking a risk comes with a chance of failure, but more importantly, it also comes with a chance of contentment, excitement and success.

How to step out of your comfort zone

If you choose to step out of your comfort zone and it feels right, even though it might be scary, here are some points to consider:

Start small – set an achievable yet challenging goal for yourself and then break the goal down into small, manageable steps and tasks.

Try something new – you may get an endorphin rush and find you actually enjoy it!

Be clear as to why you want to step outside of your comfort zone and focus on the benefits it may bring you.

Break some of your habits – challenge yourself in new ways by rethinking your routine or regular jobs and how you could perform them differently.

Tackle the tasks that make you feel uncomfortable first. Embrace the difficult things, and get comfortable with being uncomfortable.

Embrace positive self-talk – re-frame feelings of anxiety and fear with feelings of opportunity and excitement.

Own it! You are more resourceful than you know

My transition from running one hotel to a Regional Director role responsible for a number of hotels was scary yet exciting. I can recall my sense of pride and achievement, even though I was faced with taking a big step from what I knew and where I felt confident and in control to the unknown. I was mindful that I would have to learn as I went and project an air of authority and confidence.

Despite being out of my comfort zone, I positively embraced the challenge and opportunity that I had been given. I focused on my strengths and the reasons why I had been appointed and I steadily began to believe and display the confidence that others already saw in me. Small yet impactful goals and milestones for myself bridged the gaps, and I was receptive to the advice and the support that I was given. I made many mistakes but I learnt from them and didn't allow them to deter me. Over time, I found myself very much in my comfort zone once again.

If you are given an opportunity, embrace it and make the most of it. Tackle the "comfort zone" challenge head on with confidence. You are more resourceful than you know.

Building self-confidence

Tackling new challenges and pushing yourself out of your comfort zone requires confidence and courage. Throughout my career I was fortunate to be promoted into senior roles that carried much responsibility, but I sometimes felt like I was in over my head. If I had thought too much about the implications, the risks of failure and the challenges of some of the opportunities that I was presented with, I don't believe I would have taken them.

Learn to seize the opportunity and then work tirelessly to grow and develop into the role and to make it a success. It's all about building confidence and self-belief in your ability to be successful.

> "The imposter syndrome – the creeping fear that others will discover that you aren't as smart, capable or creative as they think you are – is very common. However many of us never completely shed those fears – we just work them out as they come."
>
> **Amy J Cuddy, Professor at Harvard Business School**

There are many ways to build self-confidence, and we talk about some of them later in this chapter. I recently attended a seminar by Herminia Ibarra, author of *Act Like a Leader, Think Like a Leader*, where she explained that to build self-confidence, you need to figure out how you come across as credible. How do you convey your competency to others and communicate your ideas in an authentic way?

Find it! Develop confidence

Throughout my career I was regularly required to speak publicly and make presentations. I had a fear of public speaking, lacked confidence in my ability to present with impact and authority and felt totally out of my comfort zone. My mind was imagining the worst case scenario, fearing failure, and I was convincing myself that I couldn't do it. If I presented poorly, I would be meeting my conscious expectation of myself.

Some simple yet powerful coaching techniques enabled me to become a confident and relaxed speaker. I was coached to re-frame my thoughts in a positive way and visualise myself presenting with confidence, authority and ease. I reinforced that image until I could see and experience myself doing it well. Until I could feel it. Until I was motivated and excited about it. Until I wanted to get up there and deliver. I visualised how great I would be feeling once I had presented and anchored those thoughts in my mind, replacing my thoughts of fear and negativity.

Confidence can be developed and nurtured, and you can achieve most things if you set a positive mind to it.

A quick visualisation to increase your self-confidence

Have you ever had a dream that felt so real it was almost like you had experienced the events? You know you didn't, but it feels like you did.

There is a great and powerful hypnotic confidence-building activity I'd like to share with you:

Close your eyes and focus on what it is you'd like to do with confidence. Remember, it can be absolutely anything. Now, as you breathe evenly, focusing on your out-breath, imagine the moment twenty seconds after having completed the task. Focus on the feeling of how easy and natural it felt; how strangely and wonderfully right and relaxed you were being that confident. Now practise recalling how it went, how calm and self-assured you were, "remembering" in detail how you felt and what you "said" and "did" as if you've just had that experience.

The more frequently you do this, the more you'll "trick" your brain into naturally feeling confident in this specific situation. This type of visualisation technique is used by top sports people during training and before big events, by singers and performers, by business people and anyone who needs to improve their self-confidence.

Here are my steps to confidence when faced with being out of your comfort zone:

Stop thinking about yourself – reverse the focus to what you can bring and achieve for others when you are confident in a situation. Consider how you can help them and frame things as an opportunity.

Develop positive emotions – look for what's great about the opportunity. Consider what you'll learn, how you'll develop, what new experiences you'll enjoy by getting out of your comfort zone.

Play to your strengths – start with areas where you already have confidence and build on them. Take small steps to build bigger changes. Think incrementally, you don't have to leap.

Be prepared to accept it might not work for you – develop a mindset to be comfortable with setbacks. Have the confidence to know that you can cope with things not going as well as expected.

When you develop resilience, and build your self-confidence you will be the best version of you. However, to be the best you can be you need to ensure that you and look after yourself.

Look after yourself

A certain level of stress can be a positive thing – it helps you to keep focused, and it can make you competitive and encourage action. Whenever I have to give a presentation or attend an important meeting, a sense of anxiety and a rush of adrenaline helps me to be at my best. However, dealing with the negative impact of stress is vitally important to us all, especially if we are leading a team of people. Stress and pressure is relative. We all feel it, but we react to and cope with it in different ways.

Look after yourself to be fitter, more energised, focused and attentive, and ultimately happier and more content. Leaders have to deal effectively with stress and pressure, and resilience is a key component of their ability.

The following have worked well for me:

Keep things in perspective – no matter how bad the circumstances or how big the challenge. Take comfort – you are not alone and you are most probably dealing with the situation much better than you think you are.

Stay fit and healthy – exercise and good nutrition are crucial. Exercise helps to keep emotions under control and allows you time and space to switch off. Good nutrition fuels your body and brain to work at their best.

Open up and offload – stress can worsen when you hold on to too much inside. Open up to someone you can trust who can provide an understanding ear.

Work/life balance – get the balance that works for you. Take time away from the business to recharge your batteries. Continuously working long hours without a break won't make you more productive. In fact, I believe it can jeopardise your performance.

Be organised and realistic – don't leave things to the last minute. Be prepared and prioritise the things that matter rather than setting yourself deadlines and expectations that are difficult to achieve.

Be mindful

Mindfulness is now a popular way of relaxing and handling pressure and stress, and I have met many people who feel energised yet calmed by the process.

Mindfulness is a mental skill that anyone can learn. It's the awareness that arises by paying attention, on purpose, to the present moment, non-judgementally. It is about relaxing, being aware of your thinking, feeling and sensing.

Here are three quick mindfulness tools that anyone can try:

The mindful minute – spend one minute focusing on your breathing. Set a timer if you want. If your mind wanders, guide it gently back to your breathing. Focus on breathing in and out, calmly, deeply. Try doing a mindful minute before a meeting or a stressful event to calm your thoughts and restore balance.

Dropping anchor – while sitting at your desk, ensure both feet are firmly and comfortably "planted" on the floor, anchored. Bring your attention to your feet, to the sensations and feelings. This is a great exercise to "get out of your head" and feel more connected with your body.

The three minute breathing space – this exercise has three parts. In the first minute put your attention to your current state – how your body feels and the thoughts you have. In the second minute, focus on your breathing, and then in the third minute, widen your awareness to your whole body again.

Summary

Be the best you can by embracing the leadership traits of integrity, resilience and leading by example, which will help to drive confidence both internally and externally. Take a balanced approach to decide whether your current situation is providing you with the challenge you require.

Getting the best out of yourself will provide the necessary support for you to get the best out of your team.

"Do you want to be safe and good or
take a chance to be great?"
Jack Canfield

CHAPTER 8

Get the best out of your team

> "Surround yourself with the best people you can,
> delegate authority and don't interfere..."
> **Ronald Regan, Fortieth US President**

Surround yourself with the best people

Surrounding myself with the best people has been instrumental in my success and the success of the business. I strongly believe that you are only as good as your team. Having the best people around you is like a partnership, and a successful team reflects well on you as a leader.

Find it! The best people to support you

We all need someone to rely on and to give us constant support and encouragement, whether on a personal or professional basis. Most successful managers and leaders have found that special someone who is a constant support, provides a listening ear, acts as a sounding board and can give honest and objective feedback.

You trust their judgement and they trust yours. They become your confidant. As you take on more responsibility, the indirect support that they can provide to you is invaluable and can play a large part in your success. I consider myself very fortunate to have worked alongside someone like this for the large part of my career. It's almost like having your own internal coach who knows your strengths and weaknesses, understands how you think, always makes time for you and is prepared to challenge you for your own benefit and that of the business.

Seek out the best to support you. Behind great leaders are great individuals.

Identify and recruit the best people, empower them, agree their objectives, be clear in terms of what's expected of them. Allow them to get on and deliver. Do your best not to interfere and you will find that they quickly add value to the business.

Very few successful leaders have all the knowledge, expertise and experience to run every department under their guardianship. They don't have the answers to everything, although some leaders think they do. Listen and draw on the experience and expertise of your team and build your leadership skills by learning from others. Don't shy away from recruiting strong, talented individuals – I have witnessed some leaders who have felt vulnerable and perhaps even threatened by experienced team members who were more knowledgeable than them in a particular area.

The challenge and opportunity is to get the best out of the best. Jack Welch, author and ex-Chairman of GE, was asked how he could appraise people who were smarter than he was.

He replied, "Learn from them. In the best case scenario, all your people will be smarter than you. It doesn't mean you can't lead them."

Don't fall into the trap of recruiting the best people you can find and then telling them how to do their job. I have often seen that cause frustration, resentment, and lack of motivation.

People who are focused, ambitious and results-driven have strong personalities and take more managing. They like to challenge, they're independent minded, and sometimes they're not prepared to conform. The best leaders address that, embrace their strengths, manage them in their own individual way, making them feel valued. Challenge is good. Challenge promotes development, a different way of thinking, and adds to the value and success of the business. The best people educate you; they push your boundaries. They make you "think smarter" and encourage you to make better-informed decisions, both for yourself and the business.

I was often reminded, when I became frustrated with the independent approach of an experienced, successful yet demanding team member, that those who prove to be more high maintenance and require more of your time and energy to manage are the ones who are likely to be the most successful and your most valuable assets.

Work it! Get the best out of the best

I worked alongside an executive who, I felt, resisted having strong, well-informed, challenging people as part of his team. He thrived on being in control, and I believe he felt threatened by individuals who were dynamic, experienced and more informed in any area of his function. Opportunities for personal growth and development of his team were limited.

There were high levels of turnover which led to a lack of internal succession opportunities within that department.

Many of the talented and ambitious individuals who left went on to be very successful in other businesses.

Surround yourself with the best people you can find. Embrace and encourage their strength to benefit them, you and the business. Be prepared to be challenged and learn from them. Get the best out of the best.

Identify, develop and retain talented people

Successful businesses grow, evolve and flourish by identifying, developing and retaining their talented people. Identify the high-flyers – those individuals you believe can add value to your business. Invest in them and spend time developing and coaching them to success. Retain them by offering them a clear pathway, show them they are valued and they have a future in the company, and most importantly meet their career aspirations. If leaders and businesses get this right, it can have a significant impact in terms of the long-term success of the business.

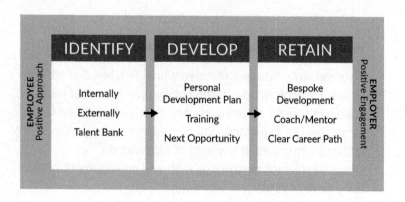

Identify talent

Identifying key people and talent is a skill, and one that should be high on the agenda for all businesses and leaders. Create your own talent bank, both internally from within your business and externally from your competitors. Identify who is working where and who the great people are, and build relationships with individuals you feel will be an asset to your business going forward. You may not currently have a vacancy, but don't wait to get that pipeline moving. Anticipate and plan ahead, so that once a vacancy arises you have potential options for replacement staff.

This talent scouting can apply to all levels of a business. You might have been served by an exceptional assistant when visiting a competitor's business. Find out a little bit more about them – how long have they worked there? What's important to them? What's their next step? Would they be interested in coming to see you? Perhaps you met a manager at a networking event and you liked their approach and professionalism. Build a relationship, make contact. Once you've opened the lines of communication, you can go back and talk to them when a suitable vacancy arises.

Work it! Be proactive

I can recall on many occasions my boss passing me the names of people to meet, research and contact, following a positive experience he'd had at another hotel or through someone he had met. I spent a great deal of my time meeting people speculatively, talking to them about their business, building a relationship, understanding a little bit about them so that we were in a position to make suitable appointments as and when the need arose. It was an approach that led to many successful appointments and was an initiative that was encouraged throughout the business.

Be one step ahead and create a potential pipeline of talent from your competitors or other businesses. Be proactive as opposed to reactive.

It's all too easy for leaders to abdicate this responsibility to the HR function or to external agencies. Successful leaders take control and ownership of this important area and adopt a more proactive approach. They network at all levels, build relationships internally and externally and encourage loyalty from both existing and future team members.

Some of the most talented people and potential high-flyers will already be in your business, but how aware of them are you? Have they gone unnoticed? It's the responsibility of all leaders at all levels of the business to identify these people and make them feel valued and recognised. A culture of regular job chats, stay interviews and performance reviews will support this process, giving both employer and employee the opportunity to get closer to one another and discuss individual aspirations. Embrace employees' strengths and their potential and develop them for the future, both for themselves, their personal growth, and for the growth of the company.

Develop and retain talent

Identifying and recruiting talented people is perhaps the easier part of the challenge. The greater challenge is to create an environment and culture that supports and encourages employee development and retention.

Development and retention go hand in hand, they are interlinked. It is widely recognised that with an improvement in the economy and an ever-growing skills shortage, retention of talent will be one of the most pressing issues for most businesses over the coming years. I believe it is imperative for businesses of all sizes to make sure they minimise the risk of highly talented people leaving for pastures new.

The most successful leaders and businesses will initiate and develop a range of joined-up strategies to retain their best people. Retaining key team members, especially the high-flyers, takes energy, commitment, focus and time, and it is important to invest heavily in them at the beginning and then continue that investment as their career develops.

How can you retain the most talented people?

Create an environment where your employees feel like assets and are valued and recognised for the part that they play in the success of the business. Provide opportunities for them to grow and learn. Let them know they have a part to play in the future of the company.

Devise an internal fast route development programme – whether bespoke to the individual or a company scheme. "Stairways to Success" which was devised and implemented by two of the best HR & Training Directors that I have worked with has proved to be an invaluable internal development programme comprising various steps of personal development and training, allowing people to identify what they're aspiring to and the steps required to get them there.

Provide a mentor for people from within the company – someone senior who is experienced, well-respected and influential and who can encourage and support their development. As part of a mentoring scheme that was introduced across the company, I was given the opportunity to mentor a potential high-flyer who was aspiring to become a General Manager. He felt recognised and valued because the CEO of the business was taking time to support him which provided him with the motivation to secure his first management appointment.

Provide additional responsibility by giving people a company project to be involved in so that they can build a network and influence on a wider scale. Invest in your most talented by recruiting a business or leadership coach to work with them on an individual basis, supporting them to achieve their potential.

Mentoring works

Mentor/mentee programmes can be rewarding and positive for everyone involved. Give staff the opportunity to have a mentor who encourages them within the business and provides them with opportunities to learn and grow; someone who understands the part they play in the company. Being a mentor allows a senior team member to take more responsibility, show the company what they're capable of doing, and create open and honest feedback. Through conversation you can support and encourage development for the mentors and mentees.

An internal mentoring scheme can add value to the mentor, mentee and the company and helps to create a culture of learning, development and retention.

Stay interviews

Ongoing conversation with employees is essential to development and retention. This is usually facilitated through job chats, reviews and appraisals. Much focus and importance is placed on carrying out exit interviews when an employee decides to leave, but how much focus is placed on "stay interviews" while the employee's still working and developing within the company?

A stay interview will offer a proactive insight into your staff – what's working for them now – and will give you some ideas of where the company can improve. Carried out on a regular basis, stay interviews make employees feel their input is appreciated, and businesses gain valuable insights into the changing needs of the employee.

Stay interviews are proactive rather than reactive, pre-empt issues and encourage employee engagement and loyalty.

During the interview it's important to be seen to be listening, and take action where appropriate. It's not just another tick box exercise. There has to be action as a result of these interviews to give them the credibility and the integrity that they deserve and to encourage and support internal recognition and retention.

Despite your best efforts to develop and retain talented people, inevitably some will leave your business. It's always going to happen.

Although an employee's decision to leave is out of our control, sometimes as leaders we only have ourselves to blame if we haven't become close enough to them to understand what they are thinking, their plans for the future and how we could support them to realise their ambitions. I have witnessed many leaders who have a tendency to adopt a defensive mode when a high-flyer decides to leave the business, abdicating themselves from the part they may have played in that decision. This is an indication of being reactive rather than proactive.

In attempts to entice staff to stay, many companies will increase remuneration packages to influence them to reverse their decision. While this might solve an immediate problem, it doesn't address the underlying cause of why the employee is thinking of leaving. Invariably it's not about the package but more about the culture, the lack of development, lack of opportunity or the way they have been managed. I have frequently seen examples where the Board has offered a greater package to retain an employee, but this has led to them feeling frustrated and intolerant towards the employee and their performance going forward.

It's important that you understand the reasons why an individual wants to leave. If you believe that it's the right decision for them, you have to let people go.

Work it! Sometime you must let great people go

When a member of my team told me they wanted to leave, I always discussed the new opportunity with them to understand their reasons for leaving. If they had a great career opportunity that I couldn't offer or match then I would not persuade them to stay. I would not promise something to entice them to stay if I didn't have 100% confidence that I could deliver it to them. Unfilled promises, whether at the appointment stage or the leaving stage, will damage the credibility and integrity of you and your organisation.

Always try to stay in touch with people after they leave to take an interest in their career going forward. You never know, even though they've left your company, there may be an opportunity to get them back in another position when something suitable comes up.

I was fortunate to have a core senior team that I worked with for over fifteen years. I can remember clearly when one member of the team came to me and said that she was leaving. I was obviously disappointed because we'd worked together for so long, but I understood the rationale for her leaving and opportunities had become limited for her in the company, and she had been offered a great job full of challenge with increased responsibility and potential for her future career. I was delighted for her, wished her well and didn't attempt to persuade her to stay, instead taking great pride in the role I had played to support her in her career.

She became exceptionally successful and is now a Joint Partner and Board Member with her new company.

Sometimes it's right to let great people go to develop and fulfil their potential.

It's important to evaluate your team continually to ensure you have the right people, in the right place, at the right time. There will be those who have come to the end of the road, who aren't developing as you would like or aren't delivering, and you need to have an honest and open conversation with them. Understand why, and possibly influence, their moving on. That's just as important as identifying people you want to stay.

Although poor performance needs to be quickly and effectively addressed, I don't believe that someone suddenly becomes unsuccessful. You don't become a bad manager overnight. If there is an issue in performance or if someone isn't doing as well as they were, that's an indicator to me that something may have changed that is impacting their performance. The easy option is to move them on, but the better leaders will try to understand the underlying issue and help them, support them, and coach them to success.

Empower your team

To get the best out of your team, you as a leader need to be a master of empowerment. Empowerment is allowing capable, motivated individuals to get on with the job. It's allowing them to make decisions and be accountable to deliver results in the best way they think possible. **It's about less control from the leader, and more about giving team members the opportunity to shine.**

Empowerment evolves over time, once the trust and confidence has been established, once the relationship has been formed. Stephen Covey, author of *The 7 Habits of Highly Effective People*, says, "Trust is the highest form of human motivation", and I've seen that throughout my career. Having trust in individuals brings out the best in them, makes them feel valued and motivated. As a result, it leads to a greater commitment to improving your results.

Effective delegation allows leaders time to step away from the "doing" so that they can spend more time on reflection, thinking strategically and leading the business. It also gives opportunity for others to grow in the business through coaching and supporting them to drive their area forward.

Delegation appears to be a quite straightforward leadership skill, but it's not always as simple as it seems. Many managers find they have a challenge with delegating to others. There are plenty of reasons why people don't or struggle to delegate:

- Some people like to keep everything to themselves, hoarding information
- They're time-constrained, so they believe it's easier to do it themselves rather than spend time showing someone else what to do
- They're a little bit insecure, and they like to be in control, to be seen to be busy and able to do everything.

When you delegate, you empower. An effective leader hands over control of a project, but at the same times keeps control through review, communication, support. To delegate effectively, choose the right task to delegate, identify the right people to delegate to and delegate in the right way.

Praise your team – again and again

It's always been important for me to get praise. I understand what it feels like, how I react to it, how it motivates me. As you grow within the business, you need to remember to show recognition and appreciation for others, and find opportunities to praise and praise again.

Praise all levels of staff in the business. It's important to recognise people who aren't customer facing, who don't get as much opportunity to display what they can do, or those in the lesser skilled roles. Everyone deserves praise and recognition, and it's the challenge and responsibility of the leader or the manager to find something positive to say about their contribution. Acknowledge it and recognise it, no matter how small or insignificant it may appear.

The impact praise has is immeasurable. It builds self-confidence in your team. They feel good and more motivated. It's a powerful leadership tool, it costs nothing and it makes everyone feel great.

There's also science behind the benefits of praise. Pride, pleasure and increased feelings of self-esteem are all common reactions to being paid a compliment or receiving positive feedback. This is because it triggers the release of dopamine, a neurotransmitter that helps control the reward and pleasure centres of the brain. As well as making us feel good, dopamine can contribute to innovative thinking and creative problem-solving at work.

It's important to note that the positive effects are relatively short-lived, and for praise to have an enduring impact on employee engagement, it needs to be offered regularly – you need to praise and praise again.

To build self-confidence in the team, focus on the positives and **catch people doing things right, rather than always catching them out doing things wrong.** Just that change of mindset will make a massive difference to the culture of a business. Appreciate people throughout the day, say something good, notice what they're doing.

While it's important to praise and praise again, so that it becomes a culture, praise has to be genuine, authentic and succinct. If it's not genuine or you overplay it, it actually defeats the object. If it's too broad and general, the recipient won't believe it. Find something genuine, and almost as soon as you recognise it, give praise.

When you have to feedback some less than positive information to an employee, which is just as important as praise, begin and end with something genuinely positive. Too much criticism will drain self-confidence and energy and will lead to a reluctance to move forward. However, don't shy away from giving negative feedback. It's all about how you frame it, about balance.

Summary

Focus your energies on getting the best out of your team. Recognise talent and embrace and nurture it through empowering, delegation and recognition.

> "My main job was developing talent. I was a gardener providing water and other nourishment to our top 750 people. Of course, I had to pull out some weeds, too."
>
> **Jack Welch**

CHAPTER 9

Coach to success and listen

"Coaching is a highly effective means of unlocking
the potential of an individual in order to maximise
performance."

John Whitmore, Author of *Coaching for Performance*

Coaching supports individuals to maximise their potential. It helps them understand where they are now, where they want to go and how to get there. A business with a strong coaching culture can achieve more through its people.

If you don't have a coaching culture in your organisation, personal growth and development for your team won't be as structured, focused or fluid. Your staff will be left to their own devices to find solutions for themselves as opposed to being supported through the process. Their goals may not be realised, objectives may not be met and they may not fulfil their own personal potential.

Why you need coaching

When a business finds itself underachieving, when employees aren't realising their full potential, managers frequently turn to performance management techniques to readdress an individual's performance. While it can be argued that the purpose of managing the performance of your team is to support and realign to improve and deliver more positive results, it can also suggest an approach of control and review, exerting pressure to improve and deliver within a set time-scale. Non-delivery of the agreed success criteria and not reaching the targets set within an imposed timescale invariably has consequences. I have seen the success of the performance management process measured solely on whether the individual was moved on from the business rather than being encouraged to improve their performance.

Coaching to success on the other hand is a positive and forward-thinking process that can significantly add value to the performance of the individual or teams being coached, with that improvement directly impacting on the performance of the business.

What is coaching?

Coaching is an interactive process between two people where the coach supports, guides and facilitates the individual's progress towards achieving their goals. Coaching can define what someone wants to achieve and help get them there faster and more easily than if they'd worked by themselves. It is a motivational and liberating process that is non-judgemental and non-directive. Coaching can also be used in group situations where the goals are less individualised and personalised and more generic and pertinent to the organisation.

Own it! Coaching – a relationship of equals

As leaders we instruct and direct individuals to achieve results throughout our team. We readily offer advice and impose our own thoughts, beliefs, recommendations and solutions to resolve a problem. A team looks up to a leader and expects us to have the experience and resourcefulness to navigate them to success.

When I began coaching I had to "unlearn" many of the attributes of leadership and stop myself from finding all the possible solutions for the individual being coached. Encouraging the coachee to gain ownership of and commitment to a solution is more important than finding it and instructing it.

Coaching is non-directive and non-judgemental, a relationship of equals.

What can coaching do for us? Coaching can:

- Develop, encourage and release the **potential** from within us
- Help us focus on the future rather than the past; on what can be done rather than what has been done
- Stop us focusing on what's wrong and instead develop new behaviours which over time can be more dominant and influence change
- Help us develop self-awareness and resourcefulness, building self-confidence to achieve more
- Encourage us to take responsibility and commit to taking action
- Be a catalyst for change
- Enable us to consider various options, to try different approaches in the way we behave or do something
- Offer quality time and space where we're listened to and understood.

Importance of coaching

Here are five ways that coaching can add value to you and your business:

Space and time is created away from the workplace and the hectic daily workload for in-depth reflection and thought gathering. A coach can act as an independent, non-judgemental sounding board and can help to structure and crystallise your thoughts and thinking patterns.

Through **skilful and effective questioning techniques** your thinking is challenged to influence change and action, helping you to close the gap between your current and your potential performance.

The process provides a **framework and structure** to support and ensure a sustained commitment to achieving your goals.

It can help to develop and influence a coaching culture throughout the organisation, enabling you to **coach performance rather than manage performance**.

A coach with a background within your industry can draw on their own experience to add advice, support and value to your thinking process and decision making.

Creating a culture of coaching

Forward-looking companies are recognising that creating a culture of coaching can support individuals, and ultimately the business, to achieve levels of performance that may not have been possible with the tried and tested methods of training courses and performance management processes.

Training at all levels of a business is critical and should continue to be a fundamental part of the learning and development strategy within the organisation. However, it is my argument that most training offered is based around the needs of the business rather than the needs of the individual, for example training in core standards, customer service, health, hygiene and safety. This type of craft training is excellent for developing staff, but for retaining them and giving individuals the opportunity to grow and develop personally, many businesses are considering more of a coaching approach.

Find it! You don't have all the answers

As a coach, it can be all too easy to think you know the answers and to lead a client to an outcome that you feel is most appropriate. I quickly learnt that coaching isn't about the coach at all; it's about the client or team member – their needs, aspirations and hopes. They have the answers and solutions within themselves, and it is the role of the coach to unearth them and allow the client to discover and embrace them for themselves.

Take time to coach your team and pull and encourage solutions from within. You don't have all the answers, but your team may well do.

Coaching is flexible and can take place at all levels of an organisation in response to the needs of the business. It is now becoming more commonplace for CEOs, MDs, General Managers and high-flyers to have a personal business coach.

Typical areas for coaching include leadership development, achieving objectives, conflict resolution and time management. Coaching can also be invaluable when an individual moves from one role to another, takes on more responsibility, or requires support to get the most out of a wider team of colleagues.

The GROW model

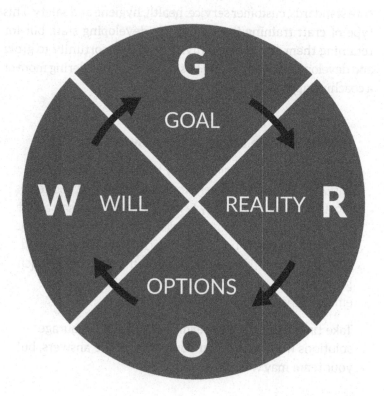

There are plenty of models around to help you on your coaching path. The simple yet effective steps to start the coaching process outlined in the GROW model are worth noting.

Goals – identify and agree an area which needs to be developed in order to benefit the individual and the business. Agree a concrete goal or objective. Once articulated, this goal will serve as a yardstick against which to measure progress and a target at which to aim. To inspire people, a goal has to focus on the future rather than dwell on the past, and it must stretch and challenge while remaining realistic. If a goal is unrealistic, it will lead to a loss of hope. If it isn't challenging enough, it won't provide sufficient motivation.

Reality – ensure the coachee has fully explained their current situation and how they feel about the areas you're focusing upon. Discover exactly what the opportunities are, what they feel is holding them back and what solutions they have already tried. A successful coach will allow the person being coached time to reflect and space to think and explain fully their current situation.

Listening is a vital part of successful coaching, but it is more complex and difficult than many people imagine. Understanding rather than just hearing is the key. Summarise what you think you've heard to confirm genuine understanding. Also try to discuss the things which aren't being said as well as those which are.

Options – Use questioning to guide the coachee towards reconsidering the relevant issues and reviewing their options. Encourage them to ask what they could have done, what steps they've considered and what they need to do to achieve their stated goals. The fact that they come up with solutions rather than having answers presented to them creates a sense of ownership.

Open ended questions are more likely to lead to greater understanding. Questions framed with "when", "what" and "who" are more effective than those based around "why" and "how". The latter may lead to the coachee adopting defensive, closed thought patterns. Incisive challenging questions will encourage the recipient to pause, reflect and examine their own thought patterns in a transformative manner, helping to draw out all the potential options for consideration.

Will and Way Forward – having been presented with options by the person being coached, you review them and set concrete actions designed to achieve the agreed goal. Gain commitment on when and how these actions will be met, and insist on highly specific answers. If needed, create a challenge by asking what could get in the way of the coachee performing the actions, and discuss relevant solutions to these hurdles. Set up a firm follow-up and review process.

Have a look at "Chapter 6: Get specific and make it happen" for more information on the Will.

As leaders and managers we have been taught to be directive, to give advice and to lead. The most effective business coaches should be able to adapt and flex their approach to suit the needs of the coachee. A good coach will be patient, offer support, listen without interruption and build a trusting relationship.

Find it! Get a great coach

My coach has had a significant impact on how I think and approach my life and my business. I have been encouraged, supported and pushed beyond what I thought I was capable of, unlocking my hopes, plans and the potential that lay within me.

Now I am coaching individuals to achieve more both personally and professionally. Challenging them to increase their self-awareness and to commit to actions that support their personal development. On reflection, I should have encouraged and influenced more of my team to have an external coach to support their growth and development and ultimately their performance.

A coach can be a powerful resource to a business and team by positively influencing the results and creating greater success.

What is mentoring?

Mentoring is another invaluable discipline to support individual growth and development, and it is my view that it can sit very comfortably within the remit of coaching.

There are clear differences between coaching and mentoring, and much time is spent in the coaching world articulating them. Mentoring is more about guiding and teaching someone in a specific task or job. The mentor will draw significantly on their own experiences, pass on short cuts and tricks of the trade and teach the mentee how to gain a specified result. They will be expected to know the answers and recommend possible solutions to a task-related situation.

A mentoring approach will **push** information, solutions and advice, whereas the coaching approach will **pull** out the capacity that people have within them, drawing on their own ideas, thoughts and plans. Both approaches support growth and focus on the individual so don't get caught up in the detail and the theory. Provide the attention, time and support to the individual to help them develop their potential, no matter what form it takes. **Don't badge it, just deliver it.**

CHECK – a tool for a more blended approach to coaching

So, if mentoring is about directing and offering your own knowledge and ideas, and coaching is about pulling that latent knowledge out of your staff, is there ever a need for a more blended approach? I believe there is. I call it "directive coaching", an approach I have successfully adopted, blending mentoring and coaching approaches dependant on the needs of the individual.

The CHECK framework acknowledges that on occasions individuals will request or potentially need a more leading and directive style. This model incorporates the key foundations of coaching – listening, challenging and exploring options. It also allows you to input knowledge to give some recommendations or provide solutions if they're relevant, and to do that in a balanced way.

The majority of opinions around the attributes of successful coaching are consistent with the non-directive approach – the coach holding back and not offering any advice, recommendations or suggestions to support the coachee in resolving their particular concern. While this approach is recognised as the cornerstone to successful coaching and is widely and effectively adopted across the coaching community, it can be argued that its translation into the workplace may not be as straightforward or effective.

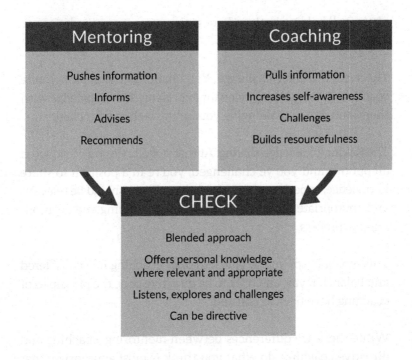

There are five steps to the CHECK framework directive coaching approach.

The **C** is for **clarify** – being clear; clarifying with your coachee their needs and expectations of you to ensure they fully understand your approach, the process, how it works and how you will support them.

The **H** is for **hold back**, for the listening stage. Give the coachee time and space to reflect and to think. You hold back on offering any views, suggestions or potential solutions at this stage.

The **E** is for **explore** and **exhaust** all the options from the coachee. You do that through effective questions. You're in the exploratory phase, still holding back and not giving any recommendations or solutions.

The second **C** is for **challenge**. You challenge the person you're coaching before sharing relevant experiences or knowledge with them, and you're challenging yourself as well as your client.

The **K** is for **knowledge sharing**. At that stage, once you've explored all options and you've challenged, you're in a position to share knowledge, experience and suggestions. These should be relevant and appropriate to support the coachee's thinking and decision-making process.

This model keeps you in check to offer coaching in a considered and balanced way, and only to be directive once the principles of coaching have been exhausted.

While there are differences between mentoring, coaching and directive coaching, do what you think is most appropriate that adds value to the person and to the business. The most important thinking is to **embrace the potential of coaching and supporting individuals and teams to success.**

The power of listening

Listening is one of the most important skills for leaders to master, but it seems that it's one that is rarely acknowledged or practised. It's possibly one of the most overlooked leadership skills. How well you listen has a major impact on your job effectiveness, your leadership ability and the quality of your relationships with others. Listening is almost like a muscle: you have to work at it to improve it and maintain its strength. **Effective listening requires education, awareness, practice and commitment.**

We all think that we are good listeners, but in reality, are we? Most people do not listen at a very deep level; they offer a superficial listening style, already thinking about what to say next or how what's being said relates to them.

"Most people do not listen with the intent to understand, they listen with the intent to reply. They're either speaking or preparing to speak. They filter everything through their own paradigms, reading their autobiography into other people's lives."
Stephen Covey, Author

Work it! Are you a good listener?

I thought I was a good listener but I now realise that I was a pretty poor one. I would be listening from my own agenda and would readily interrupt with my thoughts, recommendations and ideas. Invariably I was too busy thinking of a response and the next question to give my full attention.

It was only when I spent time studying and researching the qualities of successful coaching that I appreciated what a skill listening is. It's one that has to be understood, continually practised and mastered over time. When you consciously listen to others, you can hear so much more.

Are you as good a listener as you think you are or are you only hearing what you want?

How do we listen?

There have been a lot of studies surrounding effective listening which I believe are best summarised by Kimsey-House, explaining that there are three levels of listening.

Level 1: internal listening is all about you as an individual. "What does it mean to me?"

Level 2: focused listening, where you focus on the other person. You're observing them, you're deep in thought, listening to what they're saying. Just as importantly, you're listening to what they don't say. You're also looking at their body language.

Level 3: global listening, where you observe everything about the person. You're totally at one with that person. This level of listening activates your intuition.

Most people operate at Level 1 much of the time, but the art of listening can be learnt and developed. So, how do we become a more effective listener? What skills do we need to practise?

The effective steps to listening

Genuine listening has become a rare gift, but it can build relationships, solve and avoid problems, ensure understanding, and make everyone feel happier.

Be present – face the speaker and maintain eye contact. Turn off distractions; stop scanning the room or looking at your smartphone; genuinely be there, right now.

Relax – be attentive, be present. Keep an open mind, switch off your inner critic. Listen without jumping to conclusions.

Focus – listen to the words and allow your mind to create pictures by staying fully alert. Don't spend the time planning what to say next; think only about what the other person is saying.

Be quiet – don't interrupt. Interrupting suggests that what you have to say is more important, that you don't care what the other person has to say or that you don't have time for them. Listen patiently, even if you disagree with what they are saying.

Wait – some people speak slowly or take longer to articulate. Wait for a real stop in the conversation before speaking.

Question carefully – don't hijack the conversation with questions. Ask questions only to clarify, and avoid changing the direction unnecessarily.

Feedback – let them know you're listening. Reflect back highlights from the conversation and show you understand the sentiments.

Listening in the workplace

Even in a world of limitless instantaneous global connection, the most powerful mode of communication is that of two people listening to each other. You would think that listening to employees to get their views would be common practice, but in reality it is surprising how little **listening** happens in today's workplace.

By listening to your team members, you can tap into their creativity and learn from them, proactively asking for ideas, suggestions and feedback, which in turn encourages commitment and high levels of employee engagement. Adopting a more effective listening culture can also support your bottom line as your team will feel engaged and motivated and may well have the answers to many of your own business challenges. The worst thing an employer can do, however, is ask for input and then ignore it.

Work it! Listen to understand

I led a significant business restructure to improve productivity and streamline management. Executives who worked at a multi-site level with responsibility for several hotels were now to be hotel based, taking on the role of General Manager of a key hotel while continuing to oversee and take responsibility for further hotels.

Decisions were made with little or no discussion with those involved in the implications of the restructure. On reflection, the listening stage was overlooked as part of the decision-making process.

Views and concerns were expressed by those implicated in the change process but our desire to restructure the business as part of the evolving strategic direction of the company proved to be more important than listening to the potential implications.

The theory and rationale of the new structure seemed logical and practical, but it proved unsuccessful as many of the concerns raised became reality. Despite the significant time spent in planning and implementing it, the initiative was short-lived.

Listening is a vital stage in the decision-making process. Listen with the intent of understanding. Effective listening can make a business more efficient and profitable.

Summary

Coaching and listening can have a significant impact on getting the best out of your team and improving performance. Coach your team to success and take time to listen with an open and focused mind.

Research supports that the leaders who have the best coaching skills tend to have the better business results.

"The quieter you become, the more you can hear."

Ram Dass, Author

PART FOUR: Progress

Embrace change, push forward and consider your next steps

CHAPTER 10

Embrace change, don't fight it

> "Even if you are on the right track,
> you'll get run over if you just sit there."
> **Will Rogers, Actor**

Change is all around us, impacting both our personal and professional world. As with most things in life, you can choose to fight and resist it or you can positively embrace it, adapt to it and make it work for you. If you want to maximise your personal and professional potential then there's only one option – embrace change. Don't fight it as more often than not you won't win. Change is too powerful to resist or ignore.

Progress, personal development and career advancement are all initiated and influenced by some form of change. Opportunities will come as a result of change. Make the most of these opportunities as potential areas for growth and new experiences.

Change, however, can also cause anxiety and apprehension. It can be unsettling, creating instability and uncertainty, and while it can be positive for some it can have a negative impact on others.

Managing your own change mindset

Before you can help others through change, it is important to learn the skills and techniques to manage change yourself. These skills are easily transferable to help others.

How to help yourself and influence others through the inevitable changes:

- Create a mindset to accept that change is an integral part of life
- Remain positive while recognising and appreciating your difficulties and concerns – don't dismiss them
- Approach change situations as opportunities to grow and develop
- Demonstrate a willingness to do things differently
- Be open to any new ideas or proposals – don't immediately reject them before consideration
- Encourage others to initiate and embrace change and provide support during the process
- Communicate change in a positive manner through influencing and persuasion
- Encourage experimentation and new ways of working.

Work it! Change has implications

I have learnt a great deal from being involved in various change programmes and restructures. Some lessons have been positive, and some have been learnings from what didn't go right. One of my key learnings is that you can't expect to restructure and implement a change initiative without changing yourself, and being realistic about the implications of the change to you, others and the business.

During a restructure at both hotel and regional level, resources were significantly cut and the feedback from those affected as part of the consultation process was clear: the remaining resources at hotel level would be insufficient to cope with the various reporting requests that were initiated from head office. Time and motion studies and an analysis of the tasks to complete the basic operating requirements supported the concerns raised.

While the concerns were initially recognised and understood, they were quickly forgotten. Business carried on and the demands didn't change. From a central perspective, we were still expecting the same output from the hotels, and over time we asked for more and more to assist us in driving the business forward. Although we had changed the way the hotels were structured and operating, we didn't change our approach or expectations,

Be aware of the implications of the change process to you, your team and the business. Everyone has to play a part and be flexible to allow the change process to be effective.

Implementing change

So how do you go about making changes in a balanced and positive way? There are many models and thoughts on how to implement change, and here are three of the most recognised and widely used:

Lewin's Change Management Model – a three stage process, developed in the 1940s: Unfreeze – Change – Refreeze.

McKinsey's 7-S Framework with seven interdependent factors: Strategy, Structure, Systems, Shared Values, Skills, Style, Staff.

Hiatt's ADKAR Model of Change – five actions and outcomes: Awareness, Desire, Knowledge, Ability, Reinforcement.

We'll now take a look in a little more detail at two others, William Bridges's Transition Model and the Kotter Eight Step Change Model.

William Bridges's Transition Model

In his book *Managing Transitions*, William Bridges proposed a model focusing on transition, not change. He noted a difference: change happens to us whether we like it or not; transition is often internal.

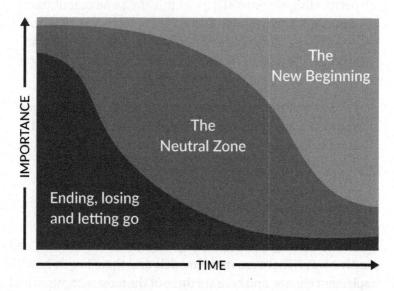

There are three stages of transition that people go through when they experience change.

Ending, losing and letting go – where there may be resistance and emotional upheaval, including anger, sadness, fear, denial, frustration and uncertainty. People need a little time to come to terms with what's happening, and it's important to talk and listen.

In a business context, ensuring everyone understands what's happening will reduce some of the fear.

The neutral zone – a period of chaos, confusion and uncertainty. This phase is the bridge between the old and the new. During this transition people may cling to the old ways of doing things, there might be resentment and scepticism with reduced productivity and anxiety. Direction and leadership is needed to boost morale.

The new beginning where people embrace change, build skills and accept the new ways of working.

Kotter Eight Step Change Model

John Kotter created an eight-step model to help businesses take a holistic approach to change so they could be more successful.

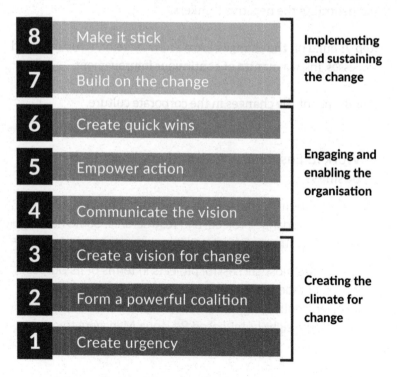

Step 1: create a sense of urgency to provide the spark and impetus to get things moving, holding open and honest communication with everyone concerned.

Step 2: form a guiding coalition, with strong leadership and a team of influential people.

Step 3: create a vision for change so everyone understands why they are being asked to do something new.

Step 4: communicate the vision, powerfully and frequently.

Step 5: encourage broad-based action, remove structural and system barriers, get rid of obstacles and empower people.

Step 6: create short-term quick wins to motivate the enthusiastic and neutralise the negative thinkers.

Step 7: build on the changes, create new systems, structures and processes, instil a mantra of continuous improvement.

Step 8: anchor the changes in the corporate culture.

Work it! Ensure change positively impacts the business

Throughout my career I have initiated and been involved with many change projects and restructures. Some have been more successful than others.

One of the most successful projects in terms of its purpose, implementation and positive impact on the business involved centralising and streamlining the revenue team from thirty-eight hotel-based Revenue Managers to a central team of just eight of the best. This team would bring their expertise, experience and best practice to support the business as a whole under the guidance and leadership of a progressive Director of Revenue.

This was a fundamental change to how the business was managed and operated; the rationale for change was very clear, well thought-out and articulated. The initial reaction to the proposed restructure was one of concern, shock and anxiety, but resistance was quickly and effectively minimised due to the strength of the business case.

This strong business case proved to be fundamental to the success of the project with both efficiency savings and incremental revenue projected. As part of a detailed communication plan, this was shared and discussed with the relevant stakeholders and the business to gain ownership and commitment to the restructure, giving confidence and credibility to the whole process.

The success of the project could also be attributed to the way we assessed, communicated with and professionally treated the relevant individuals throughout the whole process.

Have a clear purpose for change supported by a strong and well-planned business case to influence commitment and ownership from others. Ensure any change project or restructure positively impacts the business for all the right reasons.

How to support your team through the change process

If you are driving the change programme or supporting your team through it, it is important to understand how individuals are affected.

There are many reasons why people may be concerned or anxious about how the change may affect them. Often their worries are perceived as resistance and reluctance to embrace the changes.

Resistance to change can manifest itself in different ways: apathy, negativity, reduced productivity, absenteeism, etc. How you go about recognising these issues and managing them will have a major bearing on the success of your team and business.

Some best practice for managing change:

Involve as many people as you can in the planning phase so they feel they have some form of ownership of the decisions. Keep the surprises to a minimum. A perceived loss of control and dealing with the unexpected can encourage resistance.

Be clear about the process and commit to the timescales. A sense of knowing where you are with the process reduces uncertainty and creates a sense of reassurance.

Reduce defensiveness by acknowledging and celebrating past achievements. By definition, change is a departure from the past, and those who influenced the previous working practices are likely to feel defensive of what went on before.

Be honest, transparent and fair.

Be as fast as you can – don't drag things out.

Communicate to all relevant stakeholders in a consistent and timely manner.

Deliver what you promise to all impacted individuals and teams.

Appreciate and acknowledge that change is difficult and that it impacts people differently – provide support where possible and deal with individual concerns.

Use an internal or external coach to support your people through the changes.

Own it! Be open and stay positive

Change has been a constant throughout my career. I have always tried to look upon change as a positive, an opportunity to grow and develop, even when it was difficult to see it as such at the time.

Working for five different companies means I have had to be flexible, adaptable and open-minded to differing cultures, environments and leadership styles. All businesses are different with some more challenging than others.

It was the acquisition and transition process from Compass Group to Macdonald Hotels that proved to be the most challenging time for me due to the difference in size, culture and approach but on reflection it also proved to be the most exciting and rewarding.

I focused on making the most of the opportunity and actively learnt what I could from the strengths of the business while staying true to my values and style of leadership. I found that I became more rounded as a leader by embracing the change and transition, and I used it to my advantage to move up within the company and influence the culture as I went.

The benefits from change may not always be immediately clear, but keep an open and positive mind as the most challenging of circumstances may lead to unexpected and rewarding opportunities.

Don't change for change's sake

It is natural for new managers or leaders to make changes. Change in business is inevitable. There will always be changing factors, whether it's the market you operate in, the economy, the environment, or new legislation to comply to. All these factors will encourage you to flex and adapt your approach. If you don't, you, your team and your business will stagnate and fall behind the competition and market.

Leaders need to influence, predict and, most importantly, be ready and prepared for change. Great and inspirational leaders don't live in the past, retelling stories of how it used to be. They learn from the past and identify what can be helpful in the future. The way we do business, from distribution and purchasing to online working, laptops, home working, communications and social media – everything has changed and will continue to change.

However, great leaders don't make changes for change's sake, nor just to prove a point. I have seen numerous managers or individuals make changes for the wrong reasons, and the chaos and problems they caused as a result. Change has to be clear, rational, purposeful and add value to the business. Don't change things that are working well; find the opportunities and prioritise the areas that will have maximum lasting impact on the business going forward.

Own it! Don't change for change's sake

I have sometimes been accused of being resistant to change as I prefer to focus my energies on getting the most out of the status quo. I firmly believe that stability and consistency are recipes for success so long as complacency is managed and progressive thinking is encouraged, allowing the business and the team to grow and move forward together.

What I don't believe in is change for the sake of change with no real purpose or plan other than to make people feel uncomfortable and create instability, nor to implement change based solely on a personal agenda. Much time and energy can be wasted being reactive and resolving problems of change for change's sake.

Be clear about the rationale for change as otherwise you can negatively impact credibility and integrity.

Summary

Change is a constant in our world, but in all of this change there is one other constant – people. Embrace change in a balanced and positive manner, supporting and encouraging your teams to help them effectively manage the impact of change to the advantage of themselves and the business.

> "It is not the strongest or the most intelligent who
> will survive but those who can best manage change."
> **Charles Darwin**

CHAPTER 11

Maintaining momentum – consider your next steps

"If you can't fly then run, if you can't run then walk, if you can't walk then crawl, but whatever you do you have to keep moving forward."

Martin Luther King, Jr.

To be successful you need to grow and learn continually. The challenge is knowing which development efforts will yield the best results for you, your team and your business.

You might first look at your own interests and skills to see how they can be applied to business critical areas. Improve yourself to improve the business, focus on your strengths and build them. When you play to your strengths and keep passionate about learning, you will have a stronger impact on your team and the business.

Don't stand still. If you want to progress and develop your potential, then learning is a continuous cycle. Look at continuous learning in your personal life and your business life to create balance. You can't rely on your current knowledge and expertise if you expect to keep up or advance.

How do you keep progressing to reach your potential?

Continuous improvement – keep learning

The Kolb Learning Cycle is a well-practised model that is simple yet effective in its implementation. Kolb argues that we learn from our experiences of life on a continual basis, and he emphasises the importance of personal reflection as an integral part of the learning process.

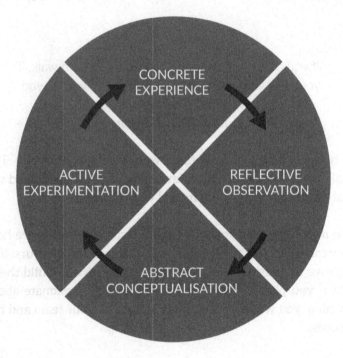

There are four stages to the cycle

Experience – in our personal and professional lives there are plenty of experiences we can learn from and use to get started on the learning cycle.

Reflect – whether you are naturally good at reflecting on your experiences or need to be a little more deliberate, this stage is vital. Take the time to think about what you've done and experienced.

Conceptualise – this is the phase where you take the reflections and interpret them to generate a hypothesis about the meaning of your experiences.

Experimentation – in this stage of the learning cycle you test the hypotheses you have generated. Your new experiences will either support or challenge these hypotheses.

Any experience has the potential to create learning, but you must take time to reflect on your experiences, interpret them and test your interpretations. This is very similar to the Visualise – Plan – Implement – Review cycle that we discussed in "Chapter 6: Get specific and make it happen". The same tools that can help you reach your goals can be used to encourage your personal development and continuous improvement.

Find it! Look for opportunities to learn

Everyone has different strengths and qualities. We can always learn something from someone – good or bad. It is just as powerful to learn what not to do as what to do.

I have always placed importance on learning from others to develop, refine and shape my leadership approach. I have been fortunate to have worked for and alongside a wealth of experienced, talented and inspirational people, and I have consciously tried to emulate a quality from all of them.

Courses, training programmes and self-help books can all add value to enhancing your leadership potential, but don't lose sight of how you can learn and develop from the wealth of people and experiences around you.

Create a learning culture

To stay relevant and be well-placed to take advantage of any opportunities, you, your team and your business critically need to influence and implement a culture of continual learning. The more progressive businesses have recognised the need to embrace a learning culture to drive and maintain strong performance and gain the competitive edge. The businesses that fail to recognise the importance of continual development and view it more as a cost than an investment are likely to experience poor levels of employee engagement and high turnover of the most talented individuals, ultimately becoming less competitive and profitable.

Creating a learning culture:

- **Increases employee engagement and motivation** which can have a direct impact on retention, customer satisfaction and productivity
- **Empowers employees to be self-directed**, giving them opportunities to grow and improve
- **Builds a "growth mindset",** encouraging employees to seek new challenges and learn from their mistakes
- **Encourages creativity and innovation** to improve productivity and overcome challenges and barriers
- **Influences positivity** across the business that encourages succession planning and career advancement.

Learning to learn is the key to driving the business forward. How do we as leaders not only embrace this need for learning but provide opportunities for employees to learn continually? How do we go about fostering the learning culture?

To influence a learning culture within your team and business:

Recognise and communicate its importance to future growth and personal development and make the culture come alive through regular initiatives.

Lead by example and commit to an ongoing plan. Demonstrate your commitment through continual investment of resources in learning, especially when the business is under-performing.

Create a coaching culture that impacts on a daily basis. Teach your managers how to coach and ask questions to build competence and confidence.

Take full advantage of on-the-job training. Learning doesn't need to be a structured training programme away from the workplace.

Make learning easily accessible. Create opportunities for on-demand and online learning, empowering employees to seek and find their own answers.

Take an active role to determine what skills need to be developed based on the needs of the individual and the business. Learning doesn't just have to relate to the business. By learning something new you are practising the skill of learning.

Encourage and reward successes and progress achieved through active learning and self-driven personal development.

When you're recruiting, look for people who have demonstrated the ability to learn new skills to advance their career. Place emphasis on recruiting and retaining lifelong learners, because even if they can't show they have the relevant skills immediately, they will be able to learn and acquire the skills they need to stay relevant tomorrow. Conversely, if they can't show their ability to learn something new, then they may not have the interest or desire to acquire the skills they need to progress.

Own it! Always be learning

Learning is a continual cycle. There is always something for you and others to learn. Having embarked on a new and exciting journey, I am very much at the learning stage again.

I can remember a clear lesson from early in my career which has always stayed with me. I was at the interview stage for a new position when I was asked to share my last valuable piece of learning and development. Struggling to answer the question, I eventually, talked about a customer service course that I had attended a while back.

I was rightly challenged about my answer, and I attempted to explain that there were only a few training courses available that year and I was waiting to be nominated for one of them. I was made to realise that I was accountable and responsible for my own learning and personal development. What had I initiated? What had I done to expand my knowledge through reading, by visiting competitors, by networking with more experienced colleagues, by reflecting on some of my experiences?

There is more to learning and personal development than attending a structured training course.

With the internet, learning opportunities are in abundance, allowing you to take the initiative. You and you alone have responsibility for your own learning and development – own it and influence it to make it count.

What skills to develop

To develop your potential, it is becoming increasingly important to focus and target your learning on the skills that are essential to progress. The challenge, given the ways in which businesses, jobs and work practices are changing, is to understand which areas of development are most important to you and which will deliver the best return to support your ambitions and objectives. The other challenge is to understand what is important to the business you are working for – where are the potential gaps that you could successfully fill through the acquisition of new skills?

I advise you to focus on three key areas:

- How you can develop your knowledge and skills to help your business become more successful
- Identify your strengths or areas of expertise and prioritise them for future development – make your strengths stronger and become more of an expert in your chosen area of expertise
- Follow your interests and passions and recognise the personal benefits to you.

Take a moment now to review the three key areas above and think about whether they are consistent with your current learning and development priorities. Reflect and prioritise your own learning plan against the criteria that is important to your personal development.

Own it! Maximise your opportunities

As the world evolves and develops, how we do business is continually changing. Working practices evolve and specialist areas emerge requiring the acquisition of new knowledge and understanding.

The way that a customer now books a hotel room has changed entirely since my days in reception and continues to evolve at a fast pace. Understanding and maximising the opportunity from a revenue and yield management perspective has now become a science and an area of expertise, providing the foundations to a successful hotel business.

Research suggests that the future hotel general managers will most likely come from a revenue management background as opposed to the traditional catering route, the most successful being those who understand the science behind revenue management. Through coaching some emerging leaders within the hotel sector, I have been greatly encouraged by their self-awareness and understanding of where to focus their energies on their own development. It is no surprise that their common theme and focus is centred around revenue management and the need to take responsibility for expanding their expertise on the subject through online courses, development programmes and immersing themselves in an area outside of their comfort zone.

Competitive advantage, whether for an individual or a business, is dependent on understanding where the potential skills and knowledge gap lies and applying that newly acquired knowledge to move forward to maximise the opportunity.

Maintaining momentum in business

Keeping a team continually motivated and focused is a key challenge for all leaders. I have been part of many new ideas, strategies, customer service programmes and sales campaigns which at the time seemed the right approach to add value and energy to the business. However, there can be a risk of overloading the business with priorities, and without a coordinated approach, momentum and the value of the initiative can quickly fade away.

Continual progress requires a disciplined approach to ensure that all areas of the business are in balance and that each is reviewed and monitored to gain maximum output. Consider reviewing business initiatives under these three areas to maximise the opportunity for and value to development and growth:

- **Start** new initiatives to drive and enhance performance in line with business priorities and to gain competitive advantage
- **Continue** maintaining momentum and getting the most out of the current initiatives
- **Stop** current initiatives that have had their day and aren't delivering value to the business anymore.

Work it! Create a buzz

I have always found that creating a buzz within your team and business helps to maintain interest and momentum. Whether it is a sales campaign, a drive to improve customer service or a vision and values exercise, the impact and longevity of the initiative is dependent on keeping it alive and meaningful in the business. Give the project a name, create an identity and influence widespread engagement by regular communication, highlighting champions and successes and getting everyone involved in some way.

"Make it your Business" was a sales-focused internal campaign that was introduced , highlighting the impact that individuals and teams can have on the sales line by consistently applying core selling standards relevant to their roles. Targets, incentives, highlighting best practice and rewarding sales champions all helped to maintain the interest and motivation which created a buzz and an energised focus across the business, driving incremental sales.

"A Commitment to Quality" initiative was also launched to support the vision and values of the company and proved to be the cornerstone and foundation to its ongoing success. Momentum was achieved through reinforcing the message at every opportunity – meetings, internal posters, online training, prompt cards and regular newsletters.

The most successful campaigns kept the initiative alive within the business and made it meaningful to everyone, recognising when it had done its job and when it was time to move on to try something new.

Create a buzz and energy around key business priorities and encourage participation at all levels through internal branded campaigns. Make them come alive, consistently reinforcing them to maximise their potential.

What next?

People often said I was like a broken record as I always conveyed and reinforced the same message at annual conferences and workshops that I fronted within the business: "The success and value of the day is solely dependent on what you do differently as a result, what actions you take." I espoused the need for **consciously doing something different to affect change and action.**

Coaching is all about change and action. It is a process that challenges how you think and how you behave to make a change and a positive difference to you, others and your business. If a particular area, a specific tool or exercise, or even an individual learning from one of my personal reflections has resonated with you, **I urge you to do something differently as a result to help you develop and fulfil the potential that surrounds you, your team and your business, no matter how big or small.**

Some suggested next steps:

- Identify and prioritise which one of the four Ps of the Dynamics of Potential model is most relevant to you
- Articulate the key learnings and what you can do as a result to make a positive difference
- Select the most appropriate exercises or tools to add value to you and your team and business
- Explore some of the areas in more detail to gain a greater understanding
- Use the book as a reference point to support and guide you on your personal and professional journey
- **Plan to make a positive difference for you, your team and your business – make it happen.**

> "People who succeed have momentum. The more they succeed, the more they want to succeed, and the more they find a way to succeed."
> **Tony Robbins, Author**

Conclusion

You can do it. Only you can release the potential within you and then help others to explore and maximise theirs.

The critical success factors of positivity, balance and the environment are fundamental to your journey, and if one of these factors is missing then the journey becomes more of a challenge and will take increased energy, compromising your ability and capacity to progress. Find them. Take ownership of them. Make them work for you.

The journey to potential will be challenging and hard work; it does not come easily. It will take personal resilience and a commitment to take action in a focused and planned way that is meaningful to your values and your goals.

Make it as easy as possible for your potential to find its own way to you. Embrace and build on your strengths and take advantage of any opportunity you are given to learn, develop and get noticed. Influence others by leading by example and through empowering and coaching to success. Your future potential is influenced by the potential of others. Your success is reflected in your team's success.

Learning and self-development is a continuous cycle. If you stop learning, you stop progressing. We all have opportunities to enhance our own performance or the way we lead our team. Task yourself with articulating your opportunities to become stronger and more successful, gaining competitive advantage to ensure you give yourself every opportunity to fulfil your potential and the potential of others.

Find it. Own it. Work it.

Although this is the end of the book, it's not the end. **Potential** is endless. It's just the beginning...

Bibliography

Jack Canfield, *The Success Principles* William Morral 2015

Professor Steve Peters, *The Chimp Paradox* Ebury Publishing 2012

Marcus Buckingham and Donald O. Clifton, PhD, *Now, Discover Your Strengths* Pocket Books 2005

Edgar Schein, *Career Anchors* Wiley 2013

Stephen Covey, *The 7 Habits of Highly Effective People* Simon & Schuster 1992

Peterson and Seligman, *Character Strengths and Virtues* Oxford University Press 2004

Herminia Ibarra, *Act Like a Leader, Think Like a Leader* Harvard Business Review Press 2015

William Bridges, *Managing Transitions* Nicholas Brealey 2003

Jenny Rogers, *Coaching Skills* McGraw-Hill 2012

John Whitmore, *Coaching for Performance* Nicholas Brealey 2014

Jack Welch, *Winning* Harper Collins 2005

Acknowledgements

I would like to thank everyone who has supported me in making this book become a reality.

In particular, Debbie Jenkins who has kept me focused during the process and provided invaluable support and advice, and Joe Gregory and Lucy McCarraher from Rethink Press. Special thanks to Stefano Philand-Maini for his support and analytical approach.

I would also like to acknowledge and express my gratitude to the people throughout my career who have given me the opportunities to take on new challenges, who have mentored and encouraged me in the process, and helped me to fulfil my own potential.

My team has been an immeasurable strength to me throughout my career and I have been fortunate to work alongside some very special people. Thank you to you all.

Finally, a big thank you to Ann and my family for your on-going support and encouragement.

The Author

As CEO for Macdonald Hotels & Resorts, the largest privately owned hotel group in the UK, from 2007 to 2014, David was responsible for over 5,000 employees and a senior executive team of twelve. Under his leadership, the company achieved successive EBITDA growth, despite the challenging economy, and was awarded the prestigious accolade of AA Hotel Group of the Year in both 2008 and 2014 in recognition of exceptional quality and customer service.

Having started as a trainee and worked his way up through all hotel departments, David rose through managerial roles before becoming CEO and Board member. In addition he has experience in both large PLCs (Forte Hotels Group, Granada and Compass) and privately owned businesses (Macdonald Hotels & Resorts). He has an exceptional range of commercial and people experience that supports the leadership development he can offer as an Executive Coach.

David completed an MBA in 2001 at Oxford Brookes University, specialising in hospitality and people management, and is a graduate of The Meyler Campbell Business School of Coaching, the leading Executive Coach training programme in the UK and accredited by the Worldwide Association of Business Coaches.

As well as holding Non-Executive roles, David is also a trustee of the hospitality based charity Room to Reward, recognising hidden heroes within the charity sector by rewarding them with hotel breaks. He has also been involved with the charity Daisy's Dream, supporting bereaved children and their families, for over twenty years.

To fulfil your Potential, subscribe to www.davidguile.com for regular newsletters, articles and leadership learnings, and to get advance notice of David's next book.

If you or a member of your team would benefit from David's direct support in your personal and professional aims, visit www.davidguile.com

To work with David on a one-to-one basis or to enquire about key note speech opportunities, email him at david@davidguile.com

Connect with David at https://uk.linkedin.com/in/dguile and https://www.facebook.com/David-Guile-Executive-Coaching-1338310476180657/

Lightning Source UK Ltd.
Milton Keynes UK
UKOW04f1431190118
316477UK00004B/72/P